AN INTRODUCTION TO THE ARCHITECTURAL HERITAGE *of*

COUNTY OFFALY

AN ROINN COMHSHAOIL, OIDHREACHTA AGUS RIALTAIS ÁITIÚIL
DEPARTMENT OF THE ENVIRONMENT, HERITAGE
AND LOCAL GOVERNMENT

Foreword

The diverse landscape and topography of County Offaly, with its vast swathes of bog, raised eskers, rivers and belts of rich farmland, had a strong influence on settlement in the county. Historical events added another dimension; and all of these factors influenced the development of the architectural heritage of the county. Architectural styles changed and evolved over the centuries and various clearly defined building types emerged.

Traces and ruins of many early religious settlements, such as the great monastery of Clonmacnoise, formed proto-urban pockets of population. Norman castles and Gaelic strongholds also attracted settlement, but urban areas did not develop beyond these small centres until the seventeenth century. By then large areas of Offaly had been planted in the first colonisation project of the modern era. Daingean and Banagher evolved from fortified sites, Fort Governor and Fort Falkland repectively.

By the eighteenth century, roads and bridges were being built to improve communication between the developing towns and neighbouring counties, and the advent of the canal brought a whole new range of building types. Hotels and inns were built to cater for the needs of passengers, warehouses to hold goods travelling back and forth on this new mode of transport. Harbours and handsome bridges marked the advance of the canal across the county until it reached the Shannon, providing a direct link from there to the metropolis of Dublin in the east. Great houses and demesnes, churches of various denominations and styles, planned towns and pretty villages, were laid out mainly during the late eighteenth and nineteenth centuries.

A view across the Offaly countryside from the windmill at Ballystrig.

NATIONAL INVENTORY
of ARCHITECTURAL HERITAGE

Offaly, probably because of the dearth of good farmland, became more industrialised than many other counties around it. Breweries and distilleries were set up, towns expanded; Clara became a centre of industry driven by the enterprising Quaker family, the Goodbodys. A legacy of gaunt industrial buildings around the county remains. Industrialisation also led to immigration, and the impact of this may be measured in the variety of churches of many denominations that were built in the county. The railways opened another chapter of building activity with stations, bridges and ancillary buildings being constructed. Austere workhouses mark the tragic years of the Great Famine. Urban development in the later nineteenth century produced the fine bank buildings and post offices that were built in some of the towns.

The advent of the twentieth century and the new state was marked by modest public building programmes: terraces of small houses for urban dwellers and individual cottages for rural smallholders, hospitals, schools and dispensaries were all built at this time. It was not until the 1950s that utilisation of the bogs on a truly industrial scale finally began and this development led to the construction of briquette factories, tall cooling-towers for the peat-fuelled power stations and housing estates for employees of both Bord na Móna and the Electricity Supply Board.

The Architectural Inventory of County Offaly was carried out in the summer of 2004. It consists of over 1000 records of buildings within the county that are deemed worthy of protection. The purpose of the survey, and this introduction to the architectural heritage, is to explore the social and historical context of these buildings and facilitate a greater appreciation of the built heritage of County Offaly.

The NIAH survey of the architectural heritage of County Offaly can be accessed on the Internet at: *www.buildingsofireland.ie*

An attractive coloured advertisement for J. & L. F. Goodbody's jute factory, dating from Autumn 1892. In 1864 the Goodbodys had built a jute factory at Clashawaun in Clara. The raw material came from India where it was spun and woven into bags and exported all over the world. Within the vignette is a view of the jute factory with chimney designed by Robert Goodbody in 1884. The chimney was built of concrete and reinforced with parts of old spinning frames from the mill. Following a lightning strike in 1962 it was reduced from 150 feet to 130 feet.

Courtesy of the National Archives.

Introduction

Raised bog near Mullaghill.

Located in the centre of Ireland and on the western edge of the province of Leinster, the most distinctive feature of the landscape of County Offaly is the extensive peatlands, including raised bogs that are spread over one-third of the county's area. Most of the land in the county is low-lying with peat laid over lime-stone, rising only to the heights of the Slieve Bloom mountains that form the southern boundary with County Laois. A raised esker (gravel ridge), known as Eiscir Riada, dominates the centre of the county. Lesser eskers provide other raised areas above the peatlands, and it was on these islands of higher ground that the towns of Tullamore and Edenderry grew up. The River Shannon and its tributaries, including the River Brosna, drain lands to the west of the county, while the River Barrow drains the south-eastern extremities. Fertile farmlands around Birr are drained by the River Camcor, while the River Boyne and tributaries mark county boundaries with Westmeath and Kildare in the north and north-east. The extensive low-lying meadows along the Shannon, called cal-lows, are submerged by the rising waters of the river each winter and provide a diversity of environments that serve as havens for wetlands wildlife.

County Offaly contains very ancient settle-ment sites dating from the Mesolithic period (7000-4000 BC). The earliest of these is situat-ed at Broughal on Lough Boora, where evidence of an ancient human presence from the pre-bog era has been uncovered. The Archaeological

Near Victoria Lock on the
Shannon Navigation in
Meelick.

(fig. 1)
**CLONMACNOISE
(founded 545AD)**

The extensive ecclesiastical site at Clonmacnoise is situated on a gravel ridge overlooking the River Shannon to the west. The archaeological remains at the site date from the Early Christian era to the close of the seventeenth century.

(fig. 2)
DURROW HIGH CROSS

A detail from the west face of the mid ninth-century Durrow high cross; on it is depicted scenes from the Crucifixion of Christ with busts of Stephaton and Longinus. This cross originally stood in the graveyard in front of St Columba's Church (c. 1733), but has now been relocated to the interior of the church.

Survey of Ireland has identified 200 ringforts, that is, farmsteads of the period AD 500-1200 defined by an earthen bank and fosse. Offaly is also rich in early ecclesiastical settlements. Clonmacnoise, on the Shannon, founded by St Ciarán, is the best known and most extensive of these and has archaeological remains that date from the mid-sixth to the end of the seventeenth century. Second only in importance to Armagh, Clonmacnoise was situated at a major crossing-point on the Shannon. A wooden bridge carrying the Slí Mhór (the Great Way) over the river was erected there in the eighth century. On this most impressive location there are three stone high crosses, two round towers and seven ruined churches in a tranquil waterside setting *(fig. 1)*. Durrow, founded by St Colmcille, is another famous monastic site known for the seventh-century illuminated Book of Durrow. It also has a high cross and some medieval and later monuments *(fig. 2)*.

Anglo-Norman settlement in the county during the late twelfth and early thirteenth centuries has left a legacy of mottes and other medieval earthworks. The visible remains of just one thirteenth-century stone castle have survived; they are situated on the western edge of the ecclesiastical site at Clonmacnoise.

The impressive and ancient Castlefield Bridge at Cadamstown, which consists of a pointed two-centred rough stone and mortar arch, dates from the fifteenth or sixteenth century and is linked to the castle nearby *(fig. 3)*. It is a very rare survivor, as implementation of the Road Act of 1727 caused many old bridges to be altered, or indeed destroyed, in order to meet the stipulation that bridges had to be wider than 12 feet.

Pre 1700

(fig. 4)
BALLYCOWAN FORTIFIED HOUSE
Ballycowan
(c. 1589 and 1626)

A complex fortified house was originally built c. 1589. Additions including a five-storey accommodation tower were added to the east side in the seventeenth century.

This area of the country remained largely in the hands of Gaelic families such as the O'Carrolls, the Mac Coghlans and others until the mid sixteenth century. During the re-conquest of Ireland, which began during the reign of Henry VIII and continued under successive Tudor and Stuart monarchs, several counties were shired. Offaly was one of these, and after it was surveyed and mapped for this purpose, became known as King's County in 1557. A policy of 'plantation' was introduced, which resulted in land grants being made to various English adventurers who came and settled in Offaly. In order to protect and consolidate the plantation scheme, a number of forts were erected. Fort Governor, founded in 1546 and later renamed Philipstown in honour of Philip II, King of Spain and consort to Queen Mary I of England, later grew into the town of Daingean. Fort Falkland, constructed in 1624, developed into Banagher.

The town of Birr was already an established settlement that had developed around the early monastery of St Brendan, before the planting of the lands of Ely O'Carroll in the early seventeenth century. Sir Laurence Parsons was granted 'the black castle, fort village and land of Birr' in 1620, when he began immediately to consolidate his position by fortifying and enlarging the gatehouse of the earlier castle. These defences were soon to be tested during the Cromwellian wars of the 1640s and '50s when Birr was besieged. However, the Parsons family retained their property and continued to prosper. The defeat of the Gaelic Irish led to more seizures and land confiscation and, during the 1650s, the transplantation of Catholics to lands situated west of the Shannon.

Towerhouses, some with bawn walls intact, are an important feature of the landscape. In Offaly, most are of sixteenth and early seventeenth-century date. Ballycowan, originally the

KNOCKARLEY HOUSE
Knockarley
(c. 1680)

Knockarley House is a good example of a transitional late seventeenth/early eighteenth-century house with its steep pitched roof, chimneystacks on the gable ends and central flat-headed doorway.

site of an O'Melaghlin castle and refurbished in 1626 for Sir Jasper Herbert, is an imposing example *(fig. 4)* and Clonony, occupied until the nineteenth century, retains its bawn *(fig. 5)*. Some of these towers have been altered from their original form and some are ruined, but several have survived reasonably intact because later dwelling houses were often attached to them. Leap Castle, originally the principal seat of the O'Carrolls of Ely, constructed in the sixteenth century, is an example of a tower that has many layers of later additions *(fig. 6)*. Other surviving examples of this type are Emmel Castle and Ballycumber House, the latter has a carved date-stone with the inscription 'Dermot Coghlan Made This Castell in Anno Dni 1627'.

A number of early houses, some dating from the mid sixteenth century, have also survived. An interesting example, dating to c. 1600, is Killeigh House, situated close to the abbey of the same name. Catholic landowners, who were later transplanted to Connacht following the Cromwellian wars, had built Ballyshiel, near Belmont, now ruined.

By 1688, that is, immediately prior to the Williamite wars, less than a quarter of the lands in Offaly remained in the hands of Catholic landowners. In the aftermath of those wars the Catholic share was reduced even further by subsequent confiscations. During the first decades of the eighteenth century there was something of a lull in Ireland, while the victorious Williamite supporters grasped the reins of administrative power more firmly. The exodus to the Continent (or, in the case of the O'Carrolls, to North America) of many of the defeated Old Irish and Old English, often with their families, added to a general slackening of pace.

(fig. 5)
**CLONONY
TOWERHOUSE**
Clonony More
(c. 1500)

An early twentieth-century view of this early sixteenth-century towerhouse. The bawn was altered during the nineteenth century.

(fig. 6)
LEAP CASTLE
Leap
(c. 1550)

Leap Castle is a sixteenth-century O'Carroll towerhouse where a Jacobean house was added to the north and later, flanking Georgian wings.

The Eighteenth Century

Established landowners, such as the Parsons of Birr and the Moores of Tullamore, who had held their lands prior to the Williamite wars, were soon able to attract new urban tenants by granting long building-leases with low ground rents that provided an impetus for the regeneration of the towns and villages in their area. While their tenants bore most of the construction costs, the landlords retained control over the type and quality of building erected on their sites. This arrangement would result in the uniform appearance of streets and layout that was to become typical of later estate towns and villages. Throughout the country a situation arose that was similar to that of the early seventeenth century. In order to protect the new, as well as the existing landowners, an extensive programme of barracks-building was undertaken. A barracks was built at Tullamore before 1717, and the earlier barracks at Daingean (Philipstown) and Banagher (Fort Falkland) were renovated.

During the first half of the eighteenth century many earlier country houses were enlarged, repaired and renovated. One of these must have been at Syngefield, near Birr, where a fine stone entrance gateway, with cut-stone piers dated to 1710, still stands. A house on the same site, dated to 1760, with classical features, is now derelict. Gloster, near Brosna is another early house; it was extensively remodelled for Trevor Lloyd, a cousin of the architect Sir Edward Lovett Pearce (c. 1699-1733), who had designed the splendid Cuba Court (now ruined) nearby. In his comments on the house, Maurice Craig states that 'the general conception is very Pearcean and sophisticated, the detailed execution less so'. Constructed in ashlar limestone, the house has a central, three-bay breakfront flanked by triple bays. Fluted Doric and Ionic pilasters in sandstone divide the side bays, and similar pilasters flank the principal doorway *(figs. 7-8)*. A carved stone door-surround has a scrolled keystone decorated with acanthus leaf. Above the doorway a segmental pediment frames the Lloyd family arms, and small, carved stone masks decorate the keystones of the window surrounds. A tall balustrade above the cornice finishes the upper storey *(fig. 9)*. Flanking two-bay extensions, with blind niches on the upper storey and tripartite windows to the side elevation, were added towards the end of the

(fig. 7)
GLOSTER HOUSE
Glasderry More
(c. 1730 and c. 1780)

Gloster House is a late
seventeenth-century
house that was extensively
remodelled c. 1730.

(fig. 8)
GLOSTER HOUSE

A flight of balustered steps
leads up to the terrace.

(fig. 9)
GLOSTER HOUSE

A tall balustered parapet
adds height to the main
block of the house.

(fig. 11)
GLOSTER HOUSE

A detail showing the coved
ceiling in the hallway.

GLOSTER HOUSE

Detail from one of the
carved keystone masks
above the window
openings.

(fig. 10)
GLOSTER HOUSE

The dramatic, double-
height entrance hall has
strongly executed niches.

century. A garden feature consisting of a rubble-stone arch flanked by obelisks is considered to be a sound attribution to Pearce and is similar to that at Arch Hall in County Meath by the same architect *(fig. 12)*. Obelisks as decorative structures were much favoured by architects in the eighteenth century and one of the finest of these, also constructed by Pearce, may still be seen in the grounds of the former Stillorgan House, County Dublin. The classical detailing on the exterior of Gloster presents a striking and unusual architectural exercise, although it is considered to be provincial in many respects. The interiors of Gloster are decorated with classical motifs that lack the finesse of detail usually associated with Pearce *(figs. 10-11)*.

(fig. 12)
GLOSTER OBELISK
Glasderry More
(c. 1730)

This arched gateway was intended as an eye-catcher to close a vista through the woods. The baroque sweep to its crown, which is pierced by an elliptical opening, the subtle projecting courses on the plinths and at the spring of the arch, all add to the picturesque effect.

GLOSTER HOUSE

Detail of the wrought-iron entrance gates.

(fig. 13)
EMMEL CASTLE
(c. 1700)

The early eighteenth-century house to the front of the towerhouse has a round-headed late eighteenth-century door-case set on a panel. The chimneystacks that project from the gable end act as buttresses to the house in a rather anachronistic late seventeenth-century manner.

A less classical but nevertheless interesting architectural ensemble may be seen at Emmel Castle, where an early eighteenth-century house was attached in an unusual manner to a large square towerhouse, previously an O'Carroll property. Rather than attaching the gable end of the house to the tower, which is the more common practice, at Emmel the house abuts the tower along its length *(fig. 14)*. The result is a pleasing blend of historic architectural styles covering the period from the sixteenth to nineteenth centuries *(fig. 13)*. Another O'Carroll tower, once their principal seat, is Leap Castle,

and here the remnants of a Jacobean house (early seventeenth century) combine with extensive additions made by the Darby family who had inherited the property through marriage to an O'Carroll heiress in the mid seventeenth century. A neo-Gothic style doorway, with flanking windows decorated with clustered sandstone colonettes and hood-mouldings in the manner of the architectural writer Batty Langley (1696-1751), has been inserted into the central tower. Flanking castellated neo-Gothic wings complete the 1760s renovations.

(fig. 14)
EMMEL CASTLE

An illustration of the junction of the early eighteenth-century house with the earlier towerhouse which occurs along its length rather than the more usual gable end union.

Many new houses built during this period were showing more interest in classical architecture. Most of the favoured designs ultimately derived from Italian architecture, which was illustrated in publications by architects such as Andrea Palladio (1508-80). Several of the larger country and town houses, influenced by architectural fashions current in England, were built in various derivatives of the classical manner. In Tullamore, then an expanding town that had developed from a small village in the early seventeenth century, substantial houses incorporating classical details were being built. The construction of a new barracks in the town and the patronage of the local landlord, John Moore, Lord Tullamore, who had built a house there before 1720, encouraged early growth. Although many older houses, such as those that make up The Bridge House, may be of early eighteenth-century date, they are concealed behind later elaborate shopfronts.

Also in Tullamore, several houses with Gibbsian doorways, a feature named after the Scottish-born architect James Gibbs (1682-1754), who had trained in Italy, may still be seen. One of these, the Round House on High Street, of about 1730, has a projecting semi-circular bay entrance with conical slated roof *(fig. 18)*. The doorway is constructed of intermittent large limestone blocks with a narrow connecting band. Such houses with semi-circular bays and Gibbsian doorways were also popular elsewhere in Offaly. Crank House (c. 1750), Main Street, Banagher, has a door-surround that has been enhanced by the addition of a skilfully curved triangular pediment with dentils and a triple Venetian window above, adding emphasis to the entrance bay *(figs. 16-17)*. Balliver House (c. 1730), formerly known as Castle Iver, has double semi-circular bays that enhance the façade of the house *(fig. 15)*.

(fig. 15)
BALLIVER HOUSE
Balliver
(c. 1730)

A fine example of double semi-circular bays flanking a carved limestone porch at Balliver House.

(fig. 17)
CRANK HOUSE VISITOR CENTRE

A detail of the elaborate and curved triangular pediment over the entrance doorway.

(fig. 16)
CRANK HOUSE VISITOR CENTRE
Main Street
Banagher
(c. 1750)

An illustration of the impressive architectural contribution this building makes to the streetscape of Banagher.

(fig. 18)
ROUND HOUSE
High Street
Tullamore
(c. 1730)

The distinctive semi-circular entrance bay features a Gibbsian door surround.

(fig. 19)
MILLTOWN PARK HOUSE
Milltown
(c. 1740)

An elegantly designed symmetrical house which utilises a number of features from the classical vocabulary. The central projecting bay has a tripartite doorway with Gibbsian doorcase, a tripartite Venetian window above, and an oculus placed centrally in the pediment.

(fig. 20)
MILLTOWN PARK HOUSE

The quadrangle of custom built farm buildings complete the setting.

(fig. 21)
MILLTOWN PARK HOUSE

A fine architectural detail from the stable block.

As the eighteenth century progressed, a more sophisticated and formal reading of architectural features was applied to many of the country houses being constructed. For instance, on the entrance front of Milltown Park House (c. 1740), which was executed in limestone ashlar, the central breakfront of three storeys has a pediment and a Gibbsian doorway approached by limestone steps *(fig. 19)*. Above the door there is a decorative fanlight and narrow flanking sidelights, while on the first floor a tripartite window, centrally placed, has an oculus above. A quadrangle of outbuildings and stables is situated to the rear of the house. This ensemble of buildings is typical of the medium-sized country house of the mid eighteenth century, and is to be seen throughout Ireland *(figs. 20-21)*.

Urban architecture was also becoming more learned, and when Cumberland Square was laid out in Birr during the 1740s, its centrepiece was a tall Doric column supporting a statue of the Duke of Cumberland *(fig. 22)*. Designed by Samuel Chearnley (c. 1717-46), it was erected in 1746 to celebrate Cumberland's victory over the Jacobites at the Battle of Culloden in Scotland. The limestone column was erected at a cost of £182.14s, and the bronzed lead statue, executed by the London sculptors John and Henry Cheere, cost £71.5.6d. Originally it was erected on ornamental rockwork and stood in an artificial lake. This arrangement was altered around 1818 and the statue, by this time in poor condition, was eventually removed in 1915, when Scottish soldiers, probably from a Highland regiment stationed at the nearby barracks, demanded that it be taken down. The square was later renamed Emmet Square in honour of the patriot Robert Emmet. Several of

SPRINGFIELD HOUSE
Ballyhugh or
Springfield
(c. 1750)

This substantial country house was built for a member of the Lucas family. The exterior lacks any classical details except for the simple triangular pediment over a central breakfront. Springfield House has fine cut stone entrance gates, outbuildings and a walled garden.

(fig. 22)
CUMBERLAND COLUMN
Emmet Square
Birr
(1746)

This view of the Cumberland column shows Emmet Square with the newly erected post office, built in 1903, in the background.

Courtesy of the National Library of Ireland.

(fig. 23)
WINDMILL
Ballystrig
(c. 1770)

Prominently sited on a hill top, in order to best utilise the wind power, the windmill, although capless and without sails, remains an attractive focal point in the Rhode landscape.

the original buildings that form three sides of the square, including Dooly's Hotel and that housing *The King's County Chronicle*, still exist, although inappropriate modern infill occupies the southern half of the west side. Cumberland [Emmet] Square was one of two open squares at either end of the long Main Street. The southern Market Square is situated in the core of the older part of the town.

The formation of the Dublin Society in 1731, later the Royal Dublin Society, helped to promote a revolution in agricultural practices. The Society also sought to provide practical guidance for landlords to improve manufacturing and other useful arts. One of its leading exponents advised that landlords would prosper if they could be persuaded to build towns on their lands. Later, the Society was to encourage development of the bogs. The landlords began to follow the example set by their counterparts in England, where money gained from agricultural sources was being invested in industry.

Evidence for early industry in the county may be seen in the remains of an ancient furnace at Shinrone, where glass was produced during the early seventeenth century. More common rural industries such as flour-milling, brewing and brick-making had also existed in earlier times but, as the eighteenth century progressed, investment in these and newer types was greatly increased. In towns such as Tullamore and Birr there is evidence for thriving tanning, wool-combing, linen and distilling industries. Edenderry had a textiles industry owned and run mainly by members of the Quaker congregation during the 1720s. The base of a windmill at Ballystrig is evidence of such industrial projects *(fig. 23)*; two further windmills were also situated in Tullamore but these were out of use by 1800.

In order to improve communications and ease travel around the country, the various County Grand Juries, made up mainly of local landowners and dignitaries, funded the build-

(fig. 24)
BELMONT BRIDGE
Bellmount or Lisderg
(c. 1750)

The bridge has pedestrian 'refuges' that rise up from the V-shaped cut waters. Two small millrace arches and a diagonally set weir, that diverts water to the nearby Belmont Mill, remind us of the industrial past.

PORTNAHINCH BRIDGE
Garryhinch
(c. 1795)

This triple-arched road bridge spans the River Barrow at the county boundary with Laois. The modest embellishments of string course and blind panels are typical of an eighteenth-century Grand Jury construction.

ing of roads. New bridges were also built as part of this initiative. At Belmont, the five-arch bridge was built in about 1750; it is a massive construction carrying a road over the River Brosna and features pedestrian 'refuges' *(fig. 24)*. Another five-arch bridge, built in about 1780 at Millgrove to span the River Figile, may have provided access for the corn-mill located nearby. The construction of a canal system connecting the Shannon and other important waterways with Dublin was seen as another scheme for improving communications, transport and trade. This was to be a major feat of engineering that entailed solving many problems caused by leakages that were encountered when the route of the canal began to cross the extensive bogs in the county. The Grand Canal had reached the borders of the county by the early 1790s and the Blundell Aqueduct of 1793, which carried the canal over the existing road in Edenderry, was one of many structures associated with this ambitious scheme *(figs. 25-26)*. A branch was constructed to link the canal with the town, where a harbour and warehouses

(fig. 25)
BLUNDELL AQUEDUCT
Edenderry
(1793)

This is the only structure in County Offaly to carry the Grand Canal over a road. It was constructed to pass over an existing route into Edenderry.

(fig. 26)
BLUNDELL AQUEDUCT

Built because the canal was constructed at a higher level than the land and roads around it. Here it can be seen to narrow as it passes through a limestone quay before it flows over the aqueduct.

THE GRAND CANAL
Edenderry
(c. 1800)

The Grand Canal with
a masonry footbridge
(c. 1802) visible in the
distant background.
This single-arch accommo-
dation bridge carries the
towpath over the entrance
to the Edenderry branch.

(fig. 27)
MOLESWORTH STREET
Daingean
(1797)

This simple but well constructed former store stands adjacent to the canal at Daingean. Together with the Molesworth Bridge (1796) and quay it forms a significant group of canal related structures.

were built. As the canal was extended westwards, several fine bridges with date-plaques mark its progress across the county. Some of the bridges were named after local landlords who contributed towards the building costs. The quay at Daingean had served as a terminus for four years before the canal was opened to Tullamore and a warehouse was built there (1797) for the storage of goods in transit *(fig. 27)*. The many bridges with associated hotels, lock-houses, harbours and warehouses are testament to the skill of the stonemasons who worked on them. Bury Bridge, built in 1799, with its elegantly lettered oval date-plaque is a good example, standing as it does at the entrance into Tullamore Harbour *(fig. 28)*. For six years the town served as the terminus for the canal until the final section reached Shannon Harbour in 1803. However,

(fig. 28)
BURY BRIDGE
Convent Road
Tullamore
(1799)

Bury Bridge carries a roadway over an entrance into the Tullamore canal dock. The bridge retains many of the typical characteristics evident in canal bridges such as the humped deck form, the mixture of finely tooled limestone and random coursed walls, and towpaths which lead under the bridge. It was erected by the Grand Canal Company and named after the owner of the Charleville Estate.

(fig. 29)
SHANNONBRIDGE
(c. 1760)

This example of a bridge keeper's house is situated at the east end of the Shannon Bridge.

because of technical difficulties caused by leakages, it was 1805 before that part was fully usable. At Shannon Harbour a complex of ancillary buildings, including another large hotel, warehouses and an agent's house, were constructed around the extensive harbour. The well-preserved keeper's house, of mid eighteenth-century date, at Shannonbridge, was built to a design by Thomas Omer (*fl.*1750-1770). These small buildings of similar appearance, with recessed arches on all four elevations, were built throughout the country, sited along the routes of the canals *(fig. 29)*.

**BOLAND'S LOCK
KEEPER'S HOUSE
Cappancur
(c. 1800)**

This is an unusual and later example of a lock house with a complex layout having three storeys on the rear elevation and two on the canal front. An oval building it has a castellated projecting porch and a curved bow to the rear.

**VICTORIA LOCK
Clonahenoge
Meelick
(1843)**

The lock was erected by the contractor William Mackenzie. Victoria Lock and associated buildings is a significant example of canal architecture. Notable for its size, the lock was built to accommodate passenger steamers. It replaced Hamilton Lock and Clonaheenoge Canal, which date from the 1750s, both of which are still present.

(fig. 30)
ST BRIGID'S CHURCH
Church Road
Clara
(1770)

This is a modest example of Church of Ireland church architecture, much enhanced by its pleasant setting.

(fig. 31)
CLAREMOUNT HOUSE
Claremount
(1793)

Panel depicting the Art
of Painting. The female
figure holds a palette and
brushes denoting her art.

(fig. 32)
CLAREMOUNT HOUSE
Claremount
(1793)

Panel depicting the Art
of Sculpture. The female
figure displays the instru-
ments of her art.

The Board of First Fruits (in operation from 1711 to about 1830) was set up to handle parliamentary funding for the building of churches and glebe houses for the Church of Ireland. St Brigid's Church in Clara was built by the Fuller family in 1770. A typical Board of First Fruits church, it is a plain building of modest proportions with a tall crenellated, four-stage tower on the west end, and stands in a churchyard *(fig. 30)*. The simple interior has a curved chancel with classical details and stained glass. A decade or so later, the Roman Catholic church of SS Peter and Paul, of similarly plain style, was built at Clyduff, near Daingean. This T-plan church has a number of unusual features: the pedimented doorcase with chamfered jambs is most striking, as are the well-carved

stone masks that have been applied to the exterior of the crenellated bell-tower. Alterations were made to the interior in the 1930s.

Towards the end of the eighteenth century, when the country was enjoying another period of prosperity, there was a surge in the building of country houses. Claremount House, built c. 1790, has some added refinements to the basic three-bay, two-storey-over-basement pattern. On the principal elevation all of its windows are larger versions of the Wyatt windows that had been used at Killagally, and an impressive porch has also been added. Two stone plaques inscribed 'Coade Londone 1793', depicting the arts of Painting and Sculpture, have been inserted over the entrance doors of the later porch *(figs. 31-32)*. The Doon, which was built c. 1800 for the Mooney family, who had been living in that area for centuries, incorporates parts of an earlier house *(fig. 33)*. The plain house has retained many original features including the sash-windows with six-over-six glazing pattern. There is a limestone Doric portico on the principal elevation, with handsome wooden door and tall sidelights that are inset with coloured glass. A distinctive carved stone arched entrance with belfry provides access to the stable-yard and there is a walled garden nearby. With its ancillary buildings, gardens, long driveway with impressive gate piers and entrance gates, The Doon forms an architecturally pleasing ensemble for a small Irish country estate.

Following the Reclaiming of Unprofitable Bogs Act of 1771, tenants were being encour-aged to drain and reclaim the boglands, where Catholics were allowed to take up long leases. Potatoes were planted on many of these small-holdings, and there was a resultant growth in the population on these marginal lands. Living conditions in this area were often very poor, with sods of peat used as walling material for dwellings. Turf was transported out of the county by barges on the newly built canals and was an important element of trade. However, there were other more ambitious schemes for draining the bogs and one, which began as early as 1800, was carried out by the multi-talented engineer, contractor and architect Bernard Mullins (1772-1850), who had worked on building the canals.

(fig. 33)
THE DOON
Doon Demesne
(c. 1800)

The austere principal façade is relieved by the addition of a Doric portico.

(34)
BALLYEGAN
(c. 1800)

This vernacular house is characteristic of the lobby entry plan with its squatness, siting relative to the road and low chimneystacks.

(fig. 35)
CLONCON
(c. 1800)

Here at Cloncon, this thatched house displays the direct-entry type with half door and small-pane timber sash windows.

The vernacular architecture of Offaly is perhaps best exemplified by the county's stock of thatched buildings. Both of the principal vernacular house types can be seen. Lobby-entry houses have a small lobby formed by a screen wall protecting the kitchen hearth from the front door *(fig. 34)* and direct-entry houses have their hearth and door at opposite ends of the kitchen *(fig. 35)*. Direct-entry houses are more numerous in the west of the county, and hipped roofs tend to be found to the east of Tullamore. Thatching techniques also change from scolloped thatching to thrust thatching as one travels eastwards. Vernacular buildings are difficult to date but surviving examples appear to date mainly to between 1750 and 1850. The majority of houses are single storey and rural. Formerly, long rows of small thatched houses

DAN AND MOLLY'S
Ballyboy
(c. 1800)

This is the only example of a traditional thatched public house remaining in County Offaly.

BALLYDOWNAN COTTAGE
Ballydownan
Geashill
(c. 1875)

The double-pile plan of this house is unique within the county.

BALLYDOWNAN COTTAGE

The sweeping of the thatch at the gables and the thatched canopy to the gable window are unusual features.

were common in the towns of Offaly but these have now been replaced by newer housing. Older vernacular roofs are notable for their timbering of tree boughs, branches and twigs. Rubble stone is used to form the walls of most of the vernacular buildings, although clay ('mud') walling gets more prevalent as one travels eastwards. At Derrinduff, near Birr, outbuildings have been incorporated into the orig-

inal house to give it long six-bay elevations. Not untypically, the house is sited at right angles to the road. At the opposite end of the scale is the diminutive house at Killurin. In a farmyard at Ballyduff South, near Ballinagar, there is a remarkable group of four thatched outbuildings, including a barn, a cowhouse and general purpose sheds, one a former house.

GLENREGAN
(c. 1800)

This limekiln survives in good condition and is a reminder of the industrial heritage of the area. Limekilns were traditionally used for the manufacture of lime for diverse needs including fertilizer for farms, and whitewash for rural buildings.

The Nineteenth Century

Although Ireland is situated on the very edge of Europe, outside events such as the American War of Independence of the 1770s and the French Revolution of the 1790s had a major impact on the politics and economy of the country. For instance, the subsequent war between England and France led to inflated farm incomes. Fears that a Napoleonic fleet would invade resulted in massive defences being constructed on or near the Shannon. Those at Meelick and Keelogue took the form of large gun batteries to guard fording places on the river. The towns of Shannonbridge and Banagher had various defensive structures, including barracks and a Martello tower, put in place to guard the river crossings. A new barracks built at Crinkle near Birr (1809), by Bernard Mullins, is said to have been large enough to house a thousand soldiers *(fig. 36)*. The Act of Union was enacted in 1800, when the Irish parliament was abolished and Ireland came under direct rule from London, although this does not appear to have had any immediate effect on the local economy. In fact it could be said that Offaly experienced a minor building boom in the first two decades of the nineteenth century with the construction of public buildings such as courthouses, schools, industrial complexes and new churches for all denominations, as well as private country houses. New roads and bridges were also being constructed at that time.

During the first decade of the century there was an upsurge in the construction of public

(fig. 36)
CRINKILL BARRACKS
Barracks Street
Crinkill
(1809-12)

Crinkill Barracks was established to provide housing for extra troops who were brought in to assist in the defence of the crossing places on the River Shannon at the time of the Napoleonic wars.

Courtesy of the National Library of Ireland.

THE BARRACKS BIRR KINGS Cᵒ. 3234 W.L.

(fig. 37)
**DAINGEAN
COURTHOUSE**
The Square
Daingean
(1807)

The principal façade of the courthouse in Daingean displays a number of classical motifs, such as niches, pilasters, pediments and roof urns, but these are applied in a fairly haphazard manner.

(fig. 38)
BIRR COURTHOUSE
Townsend Street
Birr
(c. 1830)

The castellations on this building are at odds with the austerity of the overall design.

buildings particularly those linked to the legal system. The courthouses at Daingean (1807) *(fig. 37)* and Birr (1830) *(fig. 38)* are of similar scale and share distinctive decorative features on their principal elevations; both retain some of their original timber balconies with fittings. An example of a custom-built RIC barracks (1825), still in use as a Garda station, may be seen at Clonbullogue *(fig. 39)*. The building is sited in a prominent position in the village where it presents a pleasing symmetrical façade enhanced by the retention of some original sash-windows.

(fig. 40)
THE ROYAL SHANNON
Main Street
Banagher
(c. 1800)

Another example of the centrally placed, semi-circular bay; a favoured architectural motif, widespread in County Offaly.

(fig. 39)
CLONBULLOGUE
GARDA STATION
Clonbullogue
(c. 1825)

Industrial developments included the transformation of distilling and brewing from the small domestic-scale industry of earlier decades to much larger and more commercial enterprises. The Distillery Act of 1823 introduced changes in the process by which excise duty was charged and this revolutionised the industry. The huge distillery that became Williams of Tullamore had begun in modest circumstances in the town before 1782, went out of production for a time during the early 1800s, until it was re-established in 1829. Most of the original buildings and warehouses have been demolished but some later structures are still standing. The bulk of the industry was based on processing raw materials gathered from the surrounding hinterland. There was also a large distillery at Banagher, which enjoyed a chequered career until it eventually closed in 1899, and one at Birr, established by the firm of R & S Wallace in 1806. This latter building, which was damaged by fire in 1889, has been renovated and is now in use again. Production of beer and stout also made an important contribution to the economy of the county.

If the eighteenth century had been a time for agricultural innovation and rural development, the nineteenth was to be the period of the greatest growth in urban areas. Some towns were slower to expand than others but all over the country urban development was taking place. Those small towns in the county that were served by the Grand Canal showed an early surge of development. When Samuel Lewis wrote his Directory in 1834 he numbered as many as 500 houses in the town of Banagher. One of these would have been what is now The Royal Shannon Hotel. This handsome town house (c. 1800), where the timber windows have been retained, was home to the author Anthony Trollope for three years (1841-44) when he was working for the Post Office in Ireland. Other notable features are the curved bay and distinctive, if awkward, details of the doorcase *(fig. 40)*. These elements, and a preference for extra-wide doorcases with fanlight over, run like a constant theme through the architectural heritage of the county, from the early years of the eighteenth century, through the nineteenth and in some cases into the twenty-first century.

Edenderry, where a canal spur and harbour had been completed by 1802, also grew at this time. A finely constructed combined market-house and town hall, designed by Thomas Duff, was built there in 1826 at a cost of £5,000 *(fig. 41)*. This classical pedimented building, executed in ashlar masonry, has a five-bay principal façade, with three-bay side elevations, over a rusticated ground-floor arcade. The pediment bears the arms of the Downshires. A tall lantern with clock was placed centrally on the roof. Blundell House (1813), designed by James

Brownrigg, has an admirable example of the extra-wide doorcase *(figs. 42-43)*. Built to the familiar three-bay, two-storey over basement pattern, it originally housed the Marquis of Downshire's agent. It is set behind railings and its front elevation has wide Wyatt windows and is approached by a flight of limestone steps. This house also retains former stables and other domestic offices. Other examples of the wide doorcase with fanlight of the same period are to be found in the village of Cloghan. Here a variation has been introduced where the nar-

(fig. 41)
EDENDERRY TOWN HALL
O'Connell Square
Edenderry
(1826)

This view of the former market house shows the original arcaded and open ground floors; it would have provided a focal point for the market town.

Courtesy of the National Library of Ireland.

(fig. 42)
BLUNDELL HOUSE
Fr Kearn's Street
Edenderry
(1813)

An example of a handsome townhouse that displays a wide doorway with decorative fanlight over, approached by an impressive flight of steps.

(fig. 43)
BLUNDELL HOUSE

A detail from the keystone that is an attractive feature of an outbuilding at Blundell House.

(fig. 44)
HILL STREET/
BANAGHER STREET
Cloghan
(c. 1820)

An uncommon 'waisted'
form of the wide doorway
with fanlight that was a
popular architectural motif
in County Offaly.

row sidelights have their sills well above ground level, giving a 'waisted' look to the doorways *(fig. 44)*. These substantial, well-preserved buildings provide the village with its essential character and are an important aspect of Offaly's architectural heritage. Perhaps the finest example of these architectural elements may be seen at Tullynisk House (also called Woodville) near Birr (1810), designed by Bernard Mullins as the Dower House to the Birr Castle estate. It has an extraordinarily wide entrance doorway with elliptical arch overhead and finely carved Ionic columns flanking the half-glazed door *(figs. 45-47)*. There is a splendid interior with decorative plasterwork and an unusual fireplace. Although the wide doorway was popular throughout the county, other less flamboyant designs also enjoyed popularity, such as the round-headed doorway of more moderate width situated at Emmet Street, Birr, although this example has

(fig. 45)
TULLYNISK HOUSE
(c. 1820)

Pen and wash front elevation of the house for an unexecuted design annotated as 'Chinois' of c. 1820 for 'Tullynisky Park Birr'. It shows an elegant canopied porch supported on slender columns with a smaller canopy above the central window of the first floor. It is unsigned but may be attributed to Bernard Mullins.

(fig. 46)
TULLYNISK HOUSE
Woodfield or Tullynisk
(c. 1810)

Tullynisk House possesses one of the most decorative examples of the wide doorway with fanlight over in County Offaly.

(fig. 47)
TULLYNISK HOUSE

A detail showing the glazing patterns used in the fanlight and decorative glazed door panels with side lights.

an unusual lantern feature incorporated in the decorative fanlight *(fig. 48)*.

As towns grew and prospered throughout the county, new urban buildings, some with shopfronts, were constructed. Some of these have survived. Farrells of Main Street, Clara, has retained the triple-divided shop window that was a typical feature of nineteenth-century rural shops *(fig. 49)*. The simple fascia boards and wooden pilasters flanking the window are also typical. They are set into the ground floor of a seven-bay façade that was formed by either uniting two houses or extending the original.

(fig. 48)
EMMET STREET
Birr
(c. 1830)

A detail of an unusual example of a spoked fanlight with inset lantern.

(fig. 49)
FARRELL
Main Street
Clara
(house c. 1800;
shopfront c. 1890)

A pair of timber shopfronts with tripartite display windows incorporated into this long street frontage may be dated to the end of the nineteenth century.

QUIGLEY
Main Street
Banagher
(house c. 1800; shopfront
c. 1850)

A handsome example of a substantial house with inset shopfront, which incorporates commercial architectural and decorative details of different dates. The style of the existing shopfront would suggest a late nineteent-century date, while the large windows are later replacements, as is the cement render lettering 'Merchant Tailoring' applied to the second floor.

QUIGLEY
This symmetrical shopfront has centrally placed half-glazed doors and retains many of its original features, including the cast-iron gate.

(fig. 50)
**QUAKER MEETING
HOUSE**
**Fr Kearn's Street
Edenderry
(rebuilt 1806)**

A view of the simple
exterior.

(fig. 51)
**QUAKER MEETING
HOUSE**

A view of the plain interior
with balcony.

Many churches and houses of worship were
built during the wave of church-building that
took place all over Ireland in the first half of
the nineteenth century. One of these was the
simple meeting-house (rebuilt 1806) of the
Society of Friends (Quakers) in Edenderry *(figs.
50-51)*. Still in use by that community, it stands
in walled grounds, an unpretentious building
serving as a reminder of the different strands
interwoven in our social history. Standing on
the wide and impressive Oxmantown Mall in

(fig. 52)
**BORRISNAFARNEY
CHURCH**
**Ballycormick
(1829)**

This church, behind an
enclosing wall and gates in
a quiet rural setting, is
evocative of the nineteenth
century.

(fig. 53)
**BORRISNAFARNEY
CHURCH**

A detail showing the interior
of the church with unusual
cast-iron roof trusses.

Birr, the handsome St Brendan's Church of
Ireland church was built c. 1815 to a design by
the architect John Johnson (d. 1812). The small
Church of Ireland church tucked away in the
quiet rural area of Borrisnafarney was built in
1829 with funding from Thomas Ryder Pepper
(figs. 52-53). This church is unusual for the
quality of its stonework and for the use of cast-
iron for the roof trusses. The building was constructed in two phases, with the chancel, choir
and porch being added in 1907.

(fig. 54)
ST BRENDAN'S
CATHOLIC CHURCH
Wilmer Road/
Chapel Lane
Birr
(1817-24)

(fig. 55)
ST BRENDAN'S
CATHOLIC CHURCH

Pre-dating Catholic Emancipation by several years, St Brendan's Roman Catholic church, Birr (1817-24) is another fine building designed by the architect Bernard Mullins. Lord Oxmantown, who had also donated the site, laid the foundation stone in 1817. Externally it is a large, Gothic style church of cruciform plan, with a tall steeple rising from the centrally placed western tower. The bright spacious interior has elegant galleries supported on slender columns at the west end and in the transepts; it is lit by a double row of windows to the nave *(figs. 54-55)*. Other remarkable features are the rib-vaulting and some fine stained-glass windows. An important survival is the carved marble reredos and altar dating from the mid nineteenth century. It was cleverly reconstructed in 1970-71 following the Second Vatican Council. The first of a number of buildings was constructed (1815-18) on the site of St Stanislaus Roman Catholic College at Tullybeg. It was originally built to house a Jesuit seminary and, as such, the building was a simple, well-proportioned design skilfully executed using good quality materials. Many of the original features have survived intact, including the unusual ten-over-ten glazing pattern *(fig. 56)*. Another Gothic style church, of similar date and also cruciform in plan but of very different aspect, is St Catherine's Church of Ireland church (1808-15), Hop Hill, Tullamore, designed by Francis Johnston (1760-1829) *(fig. 57)*. The church stands dramatically on a hilltop, the tall finials on the west tower increasing its theatrical aspect, while the austerity of the aisled interior is relieved by rib-vaulting and a fine east window. There is an elaborate monument in the church, dedicated to Charles Moore, Earl of Charleville (d. 1764), and executed by the London sculptor John van Nost the younger (d. 1780). This monument was originally installed in an earlier church and has been combined with a memorial commemorating John Bury who died in the same year *(fig. 58)*.

(fig. 56)
ST STANISLAUS
CATHOLIC COLLEGE
Tullybeg
(1815-18)

(fig. 57)
ST CATHERINE'S CHURCH
Hop Hill
Tullamore.
(1808-15)

This drawing depicts the
south elevation of the
church.

Courtesy of the Irish
Architectural Archive.

(fig. 58)
EARL OF CHARLEVILLE
MAUSOLEUM
St Catherine's Church
Hop Hill
Tullamore
(1764)

Situated within the church
is the marble monument
to the Earl of Charleville
carved by Jan van Nost the
younger.

Courtesy of the Irish
Architectural Archive.

(fig. 59)
CLONEYHURKE CHURCH
Crossroads
Garryhinch
(c. 1820)

The tall pointed-arched door opening with a deep chamfered surround is a distinctive feature found in many of Semple's churches.

(fig. 60)
CLONEYHURKE CHURCH

View of the interior showing the balcony and the box pews below.

(fig. 61)
WESLEYAN CHAPEL
Emmet Street
Birr
(1820)

Here the classical
pediment and Gothic
windows meet in a mix
of architectural styles.

Less grand than St Catherine's but nonetheless architecturally appealing is Cloneyhurke Church of Ireland church (1820). This church is a pared-down example of the 'spiky' Gothic style often used by John Semple (1801-82), the architect who was responsible for the design of many Board of First Fruits churches built during this period *(fig. 59)*. The interior remains largely untouched and has retained many of its original fittings, such as the carved wooden rails and box pews *(fig. 60)*. Another church with Gothic features but in a very different style is the Wesleyan Chapel in Birr (1820) *(fig. 61)*. The classical pediment evokes a temple, but the Gothic style windows with finely wrought glazing bars make a delicate contrast. In the cemetery at Borrisnafarney church, the Bloomfield family erected a mausoleum in about 1830

(fig. 62)
BLOOMFIELD
MAUSOLEUM
Borrisnafarney Church
Ballycormick
(c. 1830)

This mausoleum was
designed in the shape
of a miniature single-cell
Gothic church.

KINNITTY MAUSOLEUM
St Finnian's Church
Kinnitty
(c. 1830)

The four-sided pyramidal
mausoleum is reputed
to have been built by a
member of the Bernard
family following a visit to
Egypt. It is similar in
style and execution to
the three-sided Swifte
mausoleum located at
Castlerickard Graveyard
near Longwood County
Meath.

(fig. 62). It was designed in the shape of a miniature single-cell Gothic church with buttresses and finials on the exterior. The interior has plastered walls with bricked-up shelves for the coffins, and these have plaques bearing the names of those interred. An unusual gateway marks the entrance to the Roman Catholic cemetery at Killaderry. It is constructed of random-coursed sandstone and above the entrance there are carved limestone plaques on both faces: one is inscribed with the date 1815, both have naïve representations of the symbols of death and resurrection *(figs. 63-65)*.

(figs. 63-65)
KILLADERRY GRAVEYARD
Killaderry
(c. 1815)

This monumental gateway, which may incorporate earlier fabric, is decorated with carved plaques.

**ST COLUMBA'S
CATHOLIC CHURCH
Ballybought
(1831)**

St Columba's is regarded
as one of the finest examples of an early nineteenth-
century barn church in
County Offaly.

**ST COLUMBA'S
CATHOLIC CHURCH
Ballybought**

An interior view showing
many of the original
Gothic Revival architectural
features.

JKL STREET
Edenderry

In Edenderry a range of keystones were given individual designs.

12 OXMANTOWN MALL
Birr
(c. 1820)

A flight of stone steps lead to the handsome doorway, which has castiron seats to either side.

During the first half of the century, streets lined with fine houses were laid out in the larger towns of Birr, Tullamore and Edenderry. These towns were on lands owned by prominent landlords who took an active interest in their development, and the general layout of these urban areas retains much of the character imposed on them at that time.

'Thoughts for a Square a Tullamoore Ireland facing
The Court House

to be called "The Beaujolois"

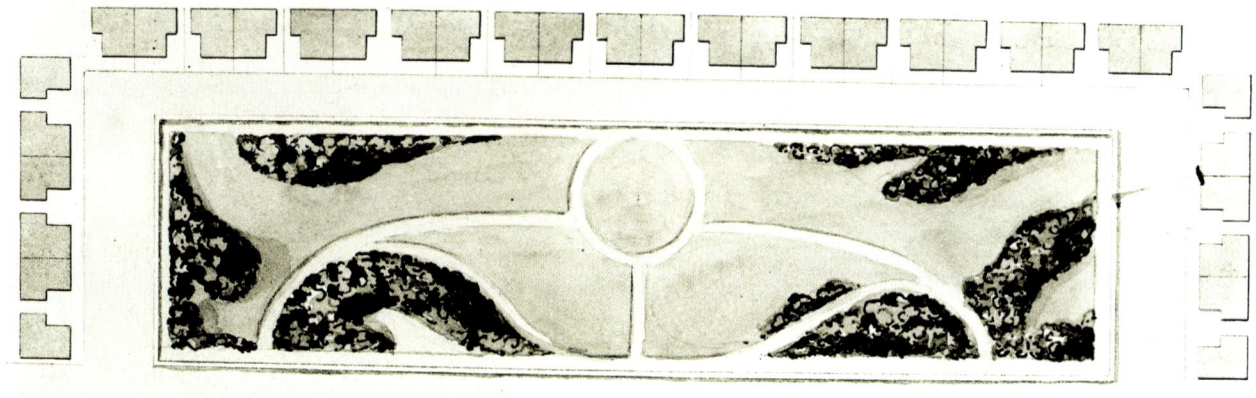

TULLAMORE
(1835)

This drawing of a proposed square, to face the courthouse, was designed by the architect William Murray and was entitled 'Thoughts for a Square at Tullamoore [sic] Ireland facing The Court House to be called "The Beaujolois"'.

Courtesy of the Irish Architectural Archive.

Areas of Tullamore had been rebuilt after a fire in 1785, when a hot-air balloon caused a major conflagration that damaged about a hundred thatched houses in the town. After the fire, the opportunity to improve the town was seized and Francis Johnston, the well-known architect, was commissioned to redesign the lower Church Street area. The increasing prominence of the town within the county may be understood from the quality and size of the gaol designed by John Killay between 1826 and 1830 and followed shortly by a courthouse (1833). Only the principal entrance and front wall have been retained at Tullamore gaol *(fig. 66)*. However, the impressive façade retains much of its former appearance. The neo-classical Tullamore courthouse, has an impressive Ionic portico and was designed by the architect John Benjamin Keane (d. 1859)*(fig. 67)*. It is similar to his Waterford courthouse. The building was damaged by fire in 1922 and rebuilt by T.F. McNamara. This distinguished building is one of the more important public buildings in the county.

(fig. 66)
KILCURTTIN
BUSINESS PARK
(TULLAMORE GAOL)
Cormac Street
Tullamore
(1826-30)

This massive gateway, executed in Norman style complete with machicolations, originally formed the entrance to Tullamore Gaol.

1-4 CORMAC STREET
Tullamore
(c. 1860)

This terrace was built to provide housing for the wardens of Tullamore Gaol.

.COVNTY.COVRTS.FOR.TVLLAMORE.

.IOHN.B.KEANE.ARCH'T.

(fig. 67)
**TULLAMORE
COURTHOUSE
Cormac Street
Tullamore
(1833)**

This drawing signed
by the architect John B.
Keane, depicts the principal elevation of Tullamore
courthouse.

*Courtesy of the Irish
Architectural Archive.*

(fig. 69)
7-8 OXMANTOWN MALL
Birr
(c. 1820)

A handsome, if austere, pair of four-bay terraced houses.

(fig. 68)
11 OXMANTOWN MALL
Birr
(c. 1820)

No. 11 is a particularly handsome example of a townhouse that retains many of its original archi-tectural and decorative features including the wrought-iron handrail bootscraper and seats at entrance level.

There was a further building campaign in Birr as the town gradually expanded northwards from the eighteenth-century Cumberland Square development. Both Oxmantown Mall, the wide thoroughfare that leads from the gates of Birr Castle to Emmet Street, and John's Place were laid out as plots during the 1820s, although some were not built on until the mid-1830s. On both streets there were variations in the types of house built, although all conform to a pleasant, if provincial, reading of the Georgian style. One pair of houses on Oxmantown Mall was built of coursed lime-stone, and the tall narrow doorways are flanked by Doric columns, supporting a narrow, fluted architrave with decorative fanlight over *(fig. 69)*. Other terraces consist of houses that utilise the extra-wide door pattern already encountered in both urban and rural settings throughout the county *(fig. 68)*. Also notable in several houses are the wooden sash-windows

(fig. 70)
JOHN'S PLACE
Birr

A view of John's Place
with John's Hall visible in
the background.

(fig. 71)
JOHN'S PLACE
Birr
(c. 1820)

An example of one of the
large detached houses on
John's Place, Birr.

CUMBERLAND TERRACE
Emmet Street
Birr
(1861)

A later example of a pair
of large townhouses,
which repeat the
Georgian pattern. Here
the central carriage arch
unites the two houses to
form a pleasing symmetri-
cal composition.

that have retained their original six-over-six
glazing pattern. John's Place is a wide, pleasant
urban space with a crescent-shaped green and
houses lining both sides *(fig. 70)*. Several of
these houses are terraced and have similar wide
doorways with columns, decorative architraves
and spoked fanlights. Original ironwork, glazing patterns and limestone steps are also in situ,
and it is the retention of these features that
gives these terraces their lasting appeal. Some
larger detached houses also feature on this
street and these repeat the Georgian pattern
with some slight variations *(fig. 71)*.

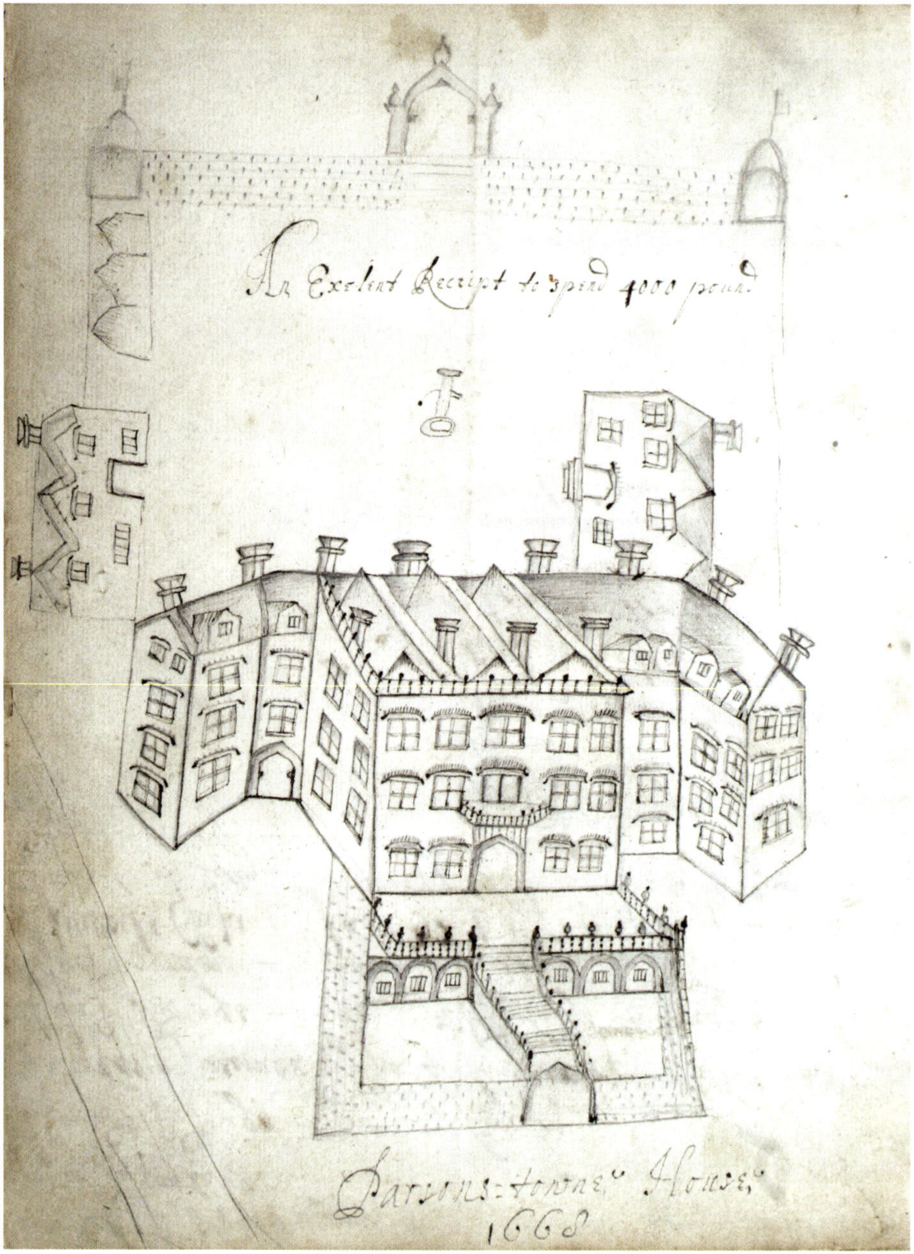

(fig. 72)
BIRR CASTLE
William Street/
Castle Street
Birr
(1668)

A drawing of 'Parsonstown House 1668', built for Sir Laurence Parsons during the 1620s and referred to by him as 'my English house'. This house was extensively altered and added to during the early years of the nineteenth century to create Birr Castle as it is today. The sketch, which is included in a Recipe Book is wittily entitled 'An Excelent [sic] Receipt to spend 4000 pound'.

BIRR CASTLE
William Street/
Castle Street
Birr
(c. 1620)

A detail from the plaster frieze that was part of the original decorative scheme in the earlier Parsonstown House. It is situated in the east flanker of Birr Castle.

(fig. 73)
**BIRR CASTLE
(1820)**

A watercolour of Birr Castle
by George Petrie is entitled
'Parsonstown Castle 1820'.
It shows the castle following the first phase of the
nineteenth-century alter-
ations, where it will be
noted that the final and
third storey has yet to be
added to the principal
front.

The two most prominent landowners who
remained resident in the county during the early nineteenth century were the Burys, Earls of
Charleville and the Parsons, Earls of Rosse;
Captain Bernard of Castle Bernard at Kinnitty
was also resident. The Digbys of Geashill, the
holders of the largest estates in the county, were
not resident and an agent was installed in the
house there. The Blundells, Earls of Downshire,
also acted through their agents. Other lesser
gentry were busy building country houses at
this time but none approached either the scale
or grandeur of the enlarged Birr Castle or the
newly built Charleville Forest. Their attached
landholdings, in the areas around Birr and
Tullamore respectively, also extended into and
influenced the development of these two
towns.

Both Birr Castle and Charleville Forest were
influenced by the prevalent fashion for
Historicism, which drew on a variety of styles
that made conscious reference to earlier architectural forms. At Birr Castle, the old house was
substantially altered and added to during the
early years of the century (1801-2), after earlier, domestic wings had been swept away
(fig. 72); and the new entrance front was dramatically emphasised by the addition of a massive three-storey central feature. This has an
inset pointed arch, mock arrow-loops, carved
stone crests and a tripartite window with central quatrefoil openings, all above the elliptical-
arched entrance porch *(fig. 73)*. In order to uni-
fy the various architectural elements, ashlar or
cut stone was applied to the façade and the
roofline was castellated. Sir Laurence Parsons,

second Earl of Rosse, and his architect John Johnston, who also designed St Brendan's Church of Ireland church (c. 1811) at the end of Oxmantown Mall, were responsible for the transformation of the earlier house into the present castle. Johnston seems to have executed working drawings from sketches prepared by the Earl of Rosse for the saloon, hall and entrance gate at the principal door of the castle. Appropriate castellated Gothic entrance gateways were also constructed and inserted in the encircling demesne walls. The interiors of Birr Castle were extensively remodelled in an eclectic variety of historical styles, mainly Gothic and Tudor Revival, at different times throughout the nineteenth and twentieth centuries. The staircase hall, which has an early staircase dating from around the mid seventeenth century, was remodelled in the Gothic Revival style with elaborate, decoratative plaster pendants, ribs and bosses, while the music room, also an addition, received a more delicate

treatment with slim colonettes supporting an airy Gothic vaulted ceiling. Horace Walpole had been one of the first to make the Gothic style fashionable in England in the form and decoration of his house, Strawberry Hill, near Twickenham, built 1750-70. But it is likely that, by the end of the eighteenth century, it was the more correct Gothic Revival style used at Fonthill Abbey, the famous house built by the architect James Wyatt (1747-1813) for his fabulously wealthy client William Beckford, that was the prime influence for the new fashion in these islands. Offaly's own Strawberry Hill, although it shares its name with the most famous and elaborate examples of the Gothic Revival house, is an altogether more modest structure, which has had a superficial layer of Gothicism applied to it. Situated at Belmont, near Birr, it is a low rambling house (c. 1810) and earlier tower of mixed architectural style, but with some pointed doorways and windows associated with the Gothic Revival style.

CHAIN BRIDGE
Birr Castle Demesne
(1826)

This small-scale, wire suspension footbridge was built over the River Camcor in the gardens of Birr Castle. Constructed during the 1820s it is possibly the earliest of its type in Europe. A similar bridge, though of smaller span was also built in the grounds of Kinnitty Castle.

(fig. 74)
CHARLEVILLE CASTLE
Charleville Demesne
(1801-12)

The extravagant Gothic Revival Charleville Castle was designed by Francis Johnston, in conjunction with its owner Charles William Bury, 1st Earl of Charleville.

Courtesy of the National Library of Ireland.

(fig. 75)
CHARLEVILLE CASTLE

Side elevation of the Gothic Revival chapel within the Charleville Castle complex.

(fig. 76)
CHARLEVILLE CASTLE

A substantial castellated gateway in a Norman style gives access to the stable complex of Charleville Castle.

Charleville Forest was designed by the architect Francis Johnston and constructed in the period 1801-12 for Charles Bury, first Earl of Charleville. Built on a green-field site, the exterior of this vast structure has several non-symmetrical towers with crenellations punctuating its roofline. Viewed from a distance across sweeping wooded parkland, the castle's towers, residential blocks and spiky form of the private chapel create a picturesque scene *(fig. 74)*. No other Gothic Revival house in Ireland approaches Charleville Forest for sheer impact, scale and detailed finish. The interiors are, if anything, even more striking, with no expense spared in the lavish application of appropriate Gothic Revival motifs, such as fan-vaulted plasterwork ceilings, wooden fireplaces and the magnificent heavy carved wooden ornament of the staircase, all intended to produce the required gloomy aspect of this style. Fine stables in matching

BUSHERSTOWN HOUSE
Busherstown
(rebuilt c. 1815)

Busherstown House is a coherent blend of different architectural styles. It was largely rebuilt c. 1815 when architectural elements from a number of periods were incorporated behind a Gothic Revival façade with terminating towers, crenellated parapet and smooth rendered finish.

Gothic Revival style were built nearby, as were a number of substantial gateways and lodges *(figs. 75-76)*. It is said that this extravagant building programme pushed the Earl of Charleville into bankruptcy and that he departed on travels to the Continent, to evade his debtors, where he died in Berlin in 1851. Interior decorations, which included wallpaper and furnishing by the influential William Morris (1834-96) were added during the 1880s. Several well-designed houses for gardeners, gamekeepers and other employees were later built on the estate.

Follies were popular garden features on estates, where they often took the form of towers. Offaly has several fine examples dating from the eighteenth and nineteenth centuries. The Gothic style octagonal structure at Toberdaly House (c. 1780), which was constructed on top of a ruined medieval tower-house and is of a type that was often used as a viewpoint or to enliven the skyline on the crest of a hill *(fig. 77)*; and the other, called Sadlier's Tower (c. 1820), on Mullagh Hill is located on a site that enjoys uninterrupted views of the surrounding countryside *(fig. 78)*. Others are

TOBERDALY HOUSE

A plaque situated near the
towerhouse.

(fig. 77)
TOBERDALY HOUSE
Toberdaly
(c. 1780)

A view showing the
octagonal gazebo above
the ruined towerhouse.

(fig. 78)
SADLIER'S TOWER
Killurin
(c. 1820)

Erected within the
demesne of Mullagh
House, this folly takes the
form of a small two-tier
circular tower. A plaque on
the wall bears the inscription that the tower was
built by Reverend Franc
Sadlier, who was Provost
of TCD from 1837-1851.

that at Busherstown House *(figs. 79-80)*, and the Belview Tower, dated 1817, originally associated with the country house of that name, which now stands on the Kilclare Demesne. This latter is based on the model of the round tower. Other types of small functional buildings often found on estates were dovecotes and ice-houses. The first housed birds for the table while the second was used for storing ice for the preservation and preparation of food *(fig. 81)*. A dovecote at Clonygowan is a handsome and sturdy two-storey structure which has four broad arches on the ground floor supporting the bird house above. Dovecotes were usually situated close to agricultural buildings, particularly granaries where the doves could feed on any scattered grain *(figs. 82-83)*.

(fig. 79)
BUSHERSTOWN TOWER
Busherstown
(c. 1810)

The folly's alignment with the southern wing of Busherstown House creates a pleasant vista from the drawing room window of the house. The tower's crenellated parapet echoes the castellated Gothic Revival design of the main house.

(fig. 80)
BUSHERSTOWN TOWER

Detail of the ornate cast-iron spiral stairs leading to the viewing platform.

(fig. 81)
GARRYHINCH
(c. 1800)

An icehouse located within the former Garryhinch House demesne. It survives relatively intact with the double-walled dome providing insulation from the sun.

(figs. 82-83)
CLONYGOWAN
(c. 1830)

This elaborate dovecote is situated in the grounds of the former Clonygowan House. It is a square structure supported on an arched lower storey.

(fig. 84)
CANGORT PARK
Cangort Park
(1807)

A handsome villa, which incorporates some distinguished design features, particularly in its interiors.

(fig. 85)
CANGORT PARK

The exterior is plain, apart from the entrance, which consists of a segmental-headed arch with a broad coved stucco surround framing a deeply recessed doorway.

(fig. 86)
CANGORT PARK

Detail of the delicate fret in Greek key design from the porch of Cangort Park.

Several notable houses designed by the prominent architect Sir Richard Morrison (1767-1849) were built in the county, including a fine villa and striking farm buildings for William Trench at Cangort Park (1807) *(fig. 84)*. Morrison was also responsible for two other houses of similar design at Bellair and Annaghmore. The design of Cangort is a variant on the popular three-bay, two storeys over basement pattern; it has a deeply recessed entrance porch with coved surround, which gives dramatic emphasis to the principal façade.

Inside, the porch is decorated by a Greek key fret and the doorcase has a decorative plaque above the glazed doors *(figs. 85-86)*. A curved bay on the east (garden) front is flanked by tall windows within recesses on the first floor. The interiors of the house are also fine and continue the elegant use of decorative elements that characterises the exteriors *(figs. 87-88)*. An unusual open-fronted rustic barn and a later, well-designed stable-block also feature at Cangort Park.

(figs. 87-88)
CANGORT PARK

Interior with fine can-
tilevered staircase that has
wrought-iron balusters.

*Courtesy of the Irish
Architectural Archive.*

Many handsome country houses in various architectural styles using the classical vocabulary were also built during this period. Ballyeighan House (c. 1834) was designed and lived in by the architect Bernard Mullins. It is of two storeys over basement, and has a recessed porch with fluted Doric columns flanked by panelled pilasters *(fig. 89)*. This impressive entrance feature provides architectural distinction to an otherwise fairly plain house. Other features include panelled pilasters that rise through two storeys on each of the four corners, a curved bay to the west elevation and wide eaves supported on twinned brackets. An elegant gate-lodge, gates and ancillary outbuildings complete this architectural ensemble. A well-proportioned pedimented classical gateway has been inserted into a wall leading into the walled garden *(fig. 90)*. It has a pulvinated frieze supported on Ionic columns and flanked by pilasters. Dungar House, designed in an Italianate manner by the architect Thomas Alfred Cobden (d. 1842) in 1839, was built about twenty five years later *(figs. 91-92)*. Of similar proportions to Ballyeighan, the house has a projecting rusticated ashlar porch with arched openings, and sits on a plinth approached by steps. Notable features also include wide eaves supported on stone brackets, strong horizontal lines that are formed by the banded string course; heavy quoins that provide emphasis at the corners are also used to frame the central upper floor window on the principal elevation. This house also has extensive stables, yards and other ancillary buildings including an interesting gate-lodge *(fig. 93)*.

(fig. 89)
BALLYEIGHAN HOUSE
Ballyegan
(c. 1834)

The Doric columns and pilasters dominate the entrance elevation.

(fig. 90)
BALLYEIGHAN HOUSE

Detail of a carved Ionic capital from the classical gateway inserted in the nearby garden wall.

(fig. 91)
DUNGAR HOUSE
Dungar
(1839)

The rusticated ashlar porch enhances the façade of Dungar House.

(fig. 93)
DUNGAR HOUSE
Dungar
(c. 1864)

An unusual gate-lodge at Dungar House, constructed in squared limestone with bracketed eaves and porch with large-scale arches.

(fig. 92)
DUNGAR HOUSE
Dungar

Detail of the decorative plaster cornice.

CASTLE BERNARD, BIRR, KINGS Co. 9955. W.L.

(fig. 94)
KINNITTY CASTLE
Castletown and Glinsk
Kinnitty
(c. 1833)

Located at the foothills
of the Slieve Bloom
mountains, Kinnitty Castle
enjoys commanding views
of the surrounding counr-
tyside.

Courtesy of the National
Library of Ireland.

(fig. 95)
KINNITTY CASTLE
Castletown and Glinsk
Kinnitty
(c. 1835)

A plain version of the
Tudor Revival style was
used for the castellated
entrance gates.

(fig. 96)
KINNITTY CASTLE
(c. 1835)

Behind the entrance
gates is a single-storey
gate-lodge with ornate
detailing and Tudor style
chimneystack.

A more eclectic style of architecture was being introduced for many new houses that were being built or refurbished throughout the county. Several of these were based on historical styles. At Kinnitty, a florid version of the Tudor Revival style was used at Castle Bernard [now Kinnitty Castle], which was constructed in about 1833 for Thomas Bernard to the designs of the architects James (1745-1829) and George Paine. Here steep gables, castellations, finials, tall chimneystacks and a variety of window types, all elements of this new style, were used *(figs. 94-96)*. Although the building was damaged by fire in 1922, it has been restored with further improvements and embellishments. At Durrow Abbey (1837), built near the site of the ancient monastery of the same name, similar elements of the same Tudor Revival style were used on the house *(fig. 97)* and associated gate-lodge designed by William Murray (1789-1849) *(fig. 98)*.

(fig. 98)
DURROW ABBEY
Durrow Demesne
(c. 1840)

Simple Gothic Revival
details enhance the plain
gate-lodge.

(fig. 97)
DURROW ABBEY
Durrow Demesne
(1837)

A view from the south-
east highlights the simple
massing of the house with
richly ornamented gable
end bays, tall chim-
neystacks, and corner
turrets of the Tudor
Revival style. Durrow
Abbey demense is a good
example of a country
house set in a historic
landscape designed in the
natural style.

(fig. 99)
**KILCLONCORKRY
HOUSE**
(c. 1820)

A small gate-lodge
with paired shouldered
windows to either side
of the doorway.

FRANCKFORT
(c. 1820)

A small but quirky exam-
ple of this type of building is the circular lodge
at Franckfort with central
chimney pot. It is known
locally as 'The Inkpot'.

Reminders of other grand houses are still to be found in interesting gate-lodges and entrance gates scattered about the county. Kilcloncorkry House gate-lodge (c. 1820) is a modest three-bay building with interesting cast-iron framed windows still in situ *(fig. 99)*.

One of the most unusual and famous structures in County Offaly, the great telescope, was constructed at Birr Castle during the 1840s for William Parsons, third Earl of Rosse. The 72-inch reflecting telescope is supported on Gothic style ashlar limestone walls. The structure underwent a major restoration in 1995. Until 1917 the Birr telescope was the largest in the world; the original mirror is now in the Science Museum in London *(fig. 100)*.

(fig. 100)
BIRR CASTLE
Birr

This watercolour by
Henrietta M. Crompton is
inscribed 'The Earl of
Rosse's work shop Birr
Castle 1852... where the
speculum was cast'.

Among the many schools built in the first half of the century, John's Hall, Birr built in 1833, is a particularly fine and unusual building *(figs. 101-102)*. It was constructed as a small temple-fronted neo-classical hall, with Ionic portico and other refined architectural features and is set in its own grounds *(figs. 103-104)*. This outstanding building was commissioned by the second Earl of Rosse to commemorate the death of a beloved son, John Clere Parsons. The grieving father stipulated that his designs for the project were '...to be executed in the best manner possible, as to render the whole chaste, harmonious and durable...' by the architect Bernard Mullins. Initially the building served as a school but it later came to be used as the town hall.

Front Elevation
of a School House, as proposed by the Earl of Rofs.

(fig. 101)
JOHN'S HALL
John's Place
Birr
(1833)

The tall doorway framed between Ionic columns of the portico of John's Hall.

(fig. 102)
JOHN'S HALL

A drawing of the proposed front elevation of John's Hall showing blind windows and railings beneath the portico.

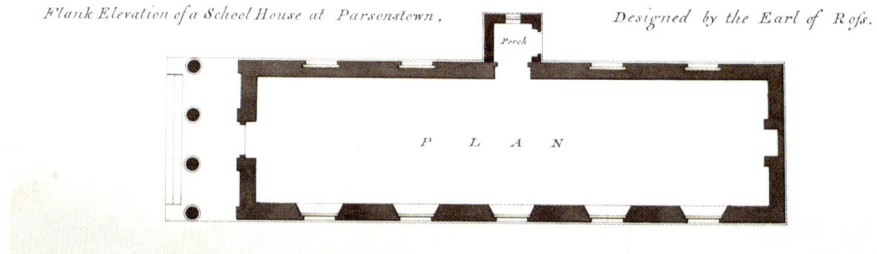

Flank Elevation of a School House at Parsonstown, *Designed by the Earl of Ross.*

PLAN

(fig. 103)
JOHN'S HALL

A drawing of the proposed side elevation and plan of John's Hall c. 1828.

(fig. 104)
JOHN'S HALL

A side elevation of John's Hall.

THE OLD SCHOOL
Bracknagh
(1843)

The old school at Bracknagh is a plain but well constructed building that combined schoolmaster's accommodation on the upper floor and school rooms downstairs. Tudor arched doorways with limestone door surrounds and cast-iron lattice framed windows set this small building in the historical revival category of architectural design.

(fig. 105)
CASTROPETRE CHURCH
Church Walk
Edenderry
(1840)

Courtesy of the National
Library of Ireland.

(fig. 106)
MARQUIS OF
DOWNSHIRE STATUE
Church Walk
Edenderry
(1846)

A view down the
driveway of Castropetre
Church, Edenderry. In
the foreground is the
limestone statue of the
Marquis of Downshire,
designed by Joseph
Robinson Kirk RHA.

In Edenderry, a dramatic entrance to the driveway of Castropetre Church of Ireland church has been created by a pair of stone gate piers, dated 1840, each surmounted by cast-iron antlered stags' heads set on a marquis's coronet *(fig. 105)*. Further up the driveway stands a monument to Arthur Blundell Sandys Trumbull Hill, the third Marquis of Downshire (1788-1845) *(fig. 106)*.

The onset of potato blight in the country in the late 1840s resulted in the Great Famine, which had a severe effect on the poorer inhabitants of Offaly. Immediately obvious were the effects on the cottiers and landless people, those who had little more than a potato garden to support them. Many perished or went into workhouses, while their often miserable hovels were levelled. Mr and Mrs S. C. Hall visited Ireland in 1840 and noted the wretched circumstances of the many turf-cutters and subsistence farmers who scraped a living on the margins of the bogs:

'It is hard to imagine more wretched hovels than those which the turf-cutter inhabits… The man usually rents from two to five acres and the turf he cuts with his own hands and conveys to market as best he can.'

Following the passing of the Poor Relief (Ireland) Act in 1838, many of the workhouses in the county were built to the designs of the architect George Wilkinson (1814-90). A large workhouse was built in Tullamore 1841 (demolished 1978) and another in about 1845 in Birr. The building in Birr has a long principal façade, the monotony of which is relieved by double-pile advanced blocks at each end and dormers in the attic storey, which have bargeboards and lattice glazing. Remarkably, the interiors of this workhouse are mainly intact and provide valuable evidence for the conditions in which inmates were housed. There is also a master's house, where the use of Tudor Revival motifs such as the steep gables, hood-mouldings and decorative glazing patterns, present an interesting historical aspect to the building *(fig. 107)*.

The Famine also affected many tenant farmers, some of whom were evicted or emigrated, leaving their abandoned dwellings dotted around the countryside as a record of this chapter of our history. Those landlords who continued to maintain an expensive lifestyle on reduced income from rents, built up debts and had to sell off their estates. Some involved themselves with the Poor-Law unions, and numerous famine-relief committees were formed. Several relief projects were set up

(fig. 107)
BIRR WORKHOUSE
MASTER'S HOUSE
Birr
(c. 1845)

Like many of the workhouses built at this time to the designs of George Wilkenson, this example displays features of a plain Tudor Revival style.

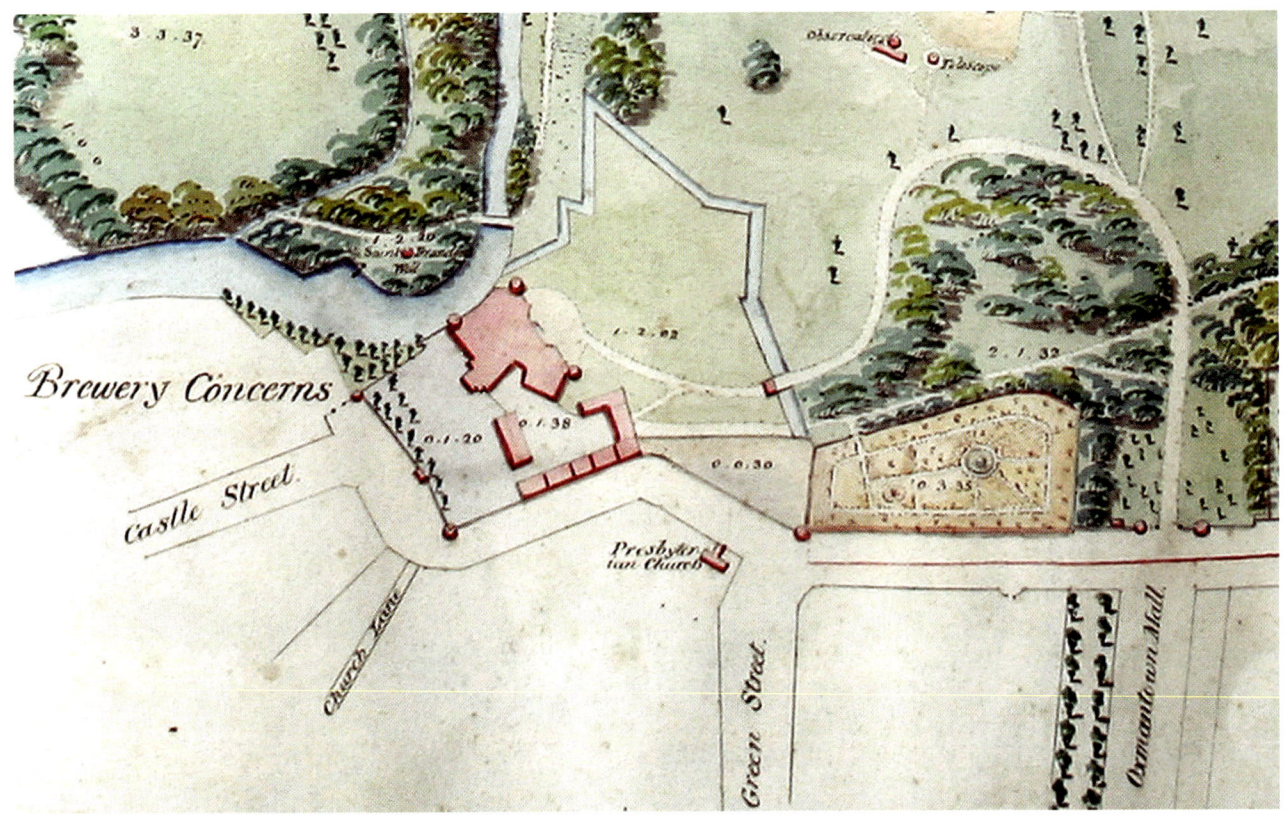

around the county, among them the excavation of a Vaubanesque moat at Birr Castle *(fig. 108)* and the construction of a gatehouse of medieval design that echoes the historicism of the recently altered façade of the castle *(figs. 110-111)*. There are architectural drawings by Mary [Field], Countess of Rosse, showing elevations

BIRR CASTLE
Birr

Detail from one of an exceptional set of detailed estate maps surveyed by John Logan, of Ormond Quay, Dublin between 1853-56, showing the extent of the star-shaped moat with the small gatehouse highlighted (in pink) guarding the entrance to the castle.

(fig. 108)
BIRR CASTLE

A view across the park
from the Vaubanesque
moat showing the castellated roofline of the castle.

O/30

East End without a chimney
Scale 10ft. to an inch.

and plans for the gatehouse in the archives at the castle *(fig. 109)*. Further building projects at Birr Castle continued throughout the 1850s and included the construction of a fine stable-block (now housing The Birr Scientific and Heritage Foundation), the rebuilding of a high boundary wall and the insertion of a set of grand castellated gates, which terminate the vista from the east down Oxmantown Mall *(fig. 112)*.

(fig. 109)
THE KEEP AND MOAT
Birr Castle
Birr
(c. 1840-45)

Design for the keep/gatehouse by Mary Countess of Rosse showing the 'East end without a chimney'. The design is thought to date from c. 1840-45.

(fig. 110)
THE KEEP AND MOAT
Birr Castle
Birr
(1840-45)

Another view of the keep/gatehouse featuring the oriel window.

THE KEEP AND MOAT

Detail showing the ornate
pattern of the iron gates
of the gatehouse.

(fig. 111)
THE KEEP AND MOAT

The keep/gatehouse built
in medieval style at Birr
Castle, designed by Mary,
Countess of Rosse.

(fig. 112)
BIRR CASTLE
Oxmantown Mall
Birr
(c. 1820)

The principal castellated
gateway in the demesne
walls of Birr Castle.

(fig. 113)
SHANNON BRIDGE
Shannonbridge
(1843)

This cast-iron twin-leaf swivel bridge originally formed the opening span to the eastern end of the sixteen-arch 1757 masonry bridge at Shannonbridge. The ingenious structure was designed by Thomas Rhodes (1789-1868) and made in 1843 by the Dublin founders J & R Mallet. It was replaced in 1984 by a reinforced concrete fixed span and is now sited on the quayside at Shannonbridge.

DERRINSALLOW BRIDGE
Bunrevan
(c. 1850)

This well proportioned bridge is a good example of a mid nineteenth-century Grand Jury presentment bridge and is quite similar to Oxmantown Bridge in Birr. It spans the Little Brosna River at the county boundary with Tipperary.

(fig. 114)
BANAGHER BRIDGE
Banagher
(1843)

Banagher Bridge is the only six-arch masonry span in the county. It replaced an earlier seventeen-arch bridge of c. 1690. Although approximately the same length as Shannon Bridge (100 metres), Banagher Bridge achieves the crossing with fewer spans, six as opposed to sixteen. It has also the longest masonry span of all of the county's bridges averaging 17.88 metres.

Improving infrastructure was also a major issue during the nineteenth century, and when the Shannon Navigation was being worked on during the 1840s, a new cast-iron swivel bridge was built at the eastern end of Shannonbridge Bridge *(fig. 113)*. Further along the river at Banagher, the earlier eighteenth-century bridge was replaced in 1843 by a wide, six-arch cut-stone structure *(fig. 114)*. The advent of the railway brought with it further expansion, easier travel and many new buildings. Paradoxically, considering that this was an innovative and modern mode of transport, historical architectural styles were adopted for several of the stations that were built at that time. Geashill railway station, built around 1856, has a stationmaster's house and ticket-office in simplified historical style, with ancillary buildings combining to form an interesting, if modest, complex from the great age of the railway in Ireland *(fig. 115)*.

BALLYCUMBER BRIDGE
Ballycumber
(c. 1850)

Originally a late eigh-teenth/early nineteenth-century bridge that was replaced by the present segmental arch in the 1850s by the Board of Works during the Brosna Drainage Scheme. Apart from Banagher Bridge over the River Shannon, this is the widest masonry arch span in the county at 12.9 metres.

KILCUMBER BRIDGE
Kilcumber
(c. 1850)

Originally a late eigh-teenth/early nineteenth-century twin arch road bridge over the River Figile. The style of the present bridge suggests a mid nineteenth-century replacement by the Board of Works as part of the Barrow Drainage Scheme. It is a well constructed and embellished bridge.

(fig. 115)
GEASHILL RAILWAY STATION
Ard
(c. 1856)

Like most small railway stations, the buildings at Geashill were built in a plain Tudor Revival style.

GAOL BRIDGE
Tullamore
(c. 1859)

This single-arch railway bridge carries the Tullamore-Kilcormac road over the Portarlington-Athlone railway line. It was erected by the Great Southern and Western Railway Company.

TULLAMORE RAILWAY STATION
Tullamore
(c. 1855)

The signal house, railway station and pedestrian footbridge form a group of related structures with the nearby railway bridge. The footbridge was made in the Dundalk foundry of E. Manisty.

(fig. 116)
ST JOHN'S CONVENT
OF MERCY
Wilmer Road
Birr
(c. 1850)

A fine complex of build-
ings partly built to the
designs of Augustus Welby
Northmore Pugin.

*Courtesy of the National
Library of Ireland.*

As the countryside settled down after the tri-
als of the Famine, more schools and churches
serving all denominations were built. In Birr
two major developments included St John's
Convent of Mercy in Wilmer Road, designed by
the famous architect Augustus Welby Pugin
(1812-52) in about 1850 for his friend, an
English nun called Sister Beckett, and the large
Parsonstown model national school (c. 1860)
designed by Jacob Owen (1778-1870). Catherine
McAuley, founder of the Order of Mercy nuns,
had visited Birr in the 1840s and the construction of the convent was begun in 1845 and
completed some eleven years later. Pugin, a
convert to Catholicism, promoted a rich style

based on Gothic architecture of the thirteenth and fourteenth centuries. Often his designs were so elaborate and archaeologically correct that they were not executed on the grounds of cost, and this is what happened here. The convent at Birr, one of the least known of his designs, displays many of the forms and details for which he was justly famous. Here one may appreciate the pairing and variety of windows, the correctly executed and elaborately carved stone mullions of the canted bay window, the fine stained glass and the well-wrought iron hinges *(fig. 117)*. However, only two sides of the cloister were complete on Pugin's death. The south range, with its staircase turret, and the eastern range with chapel were not finished until seven years after his death, and these were not to the original design *(fig. 116)*. The well-known architect George Coppinger Ashlin (1837-1921), Pugin's son-in-law, completed the chancel and the orphanage building, the monotonous rhythms of which are in sharp contrast with the harmonious massing of the original designs. This complex of buildings is undoubtedly amongst the most important architectural ensembles in the town of Birr.

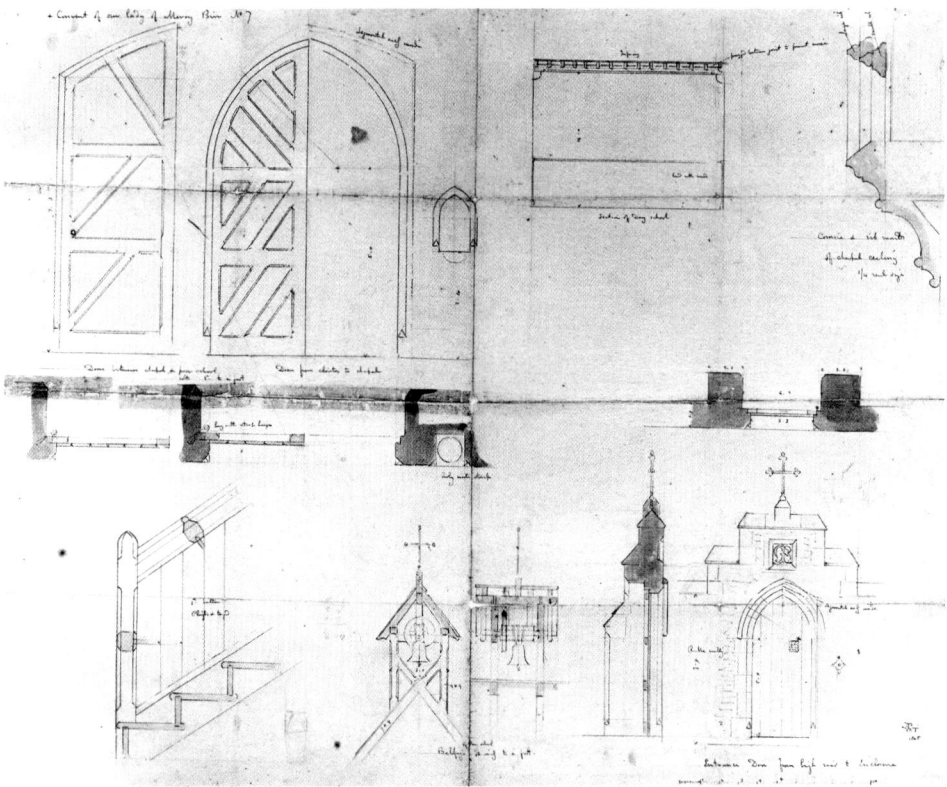

(fig. 117)
**ST JOHN'S CONVENT
OF MERCY**
Wilmer Road
Birr
(1845)

This drawing, dated 1845, shows A.W.N. Pugin's design and specifications for some of the convent's lesser architectural features.

Courtesy of the Irish Architectural Archive.

(fig. 118)
**PARSONSTOWN MODEL
NATIONAL SCHOOL**
Model School Road
(1860)

By clever use of window
types and projecting pavilions, the designer of this
building added variety
and interest to the normal
tripartite pattern for
schools of the time.

(fig. 119)
**PARSONSTOWN MODEL
NATIONAL SCHOOL**

A detail showing the skill-
ful stone carving over this
group of windows and
doorway.

(fig. 120)
GEASHILL NATIONAL
SCHOOL
Geashill
(1862)

This picturesque school
building was designed
by the architect John
Townshend Trench.

The Model School in Birr was custom built in 1860 and provides an interesting architectural essay in form and finish *(fig. 118)*. There is variety in the round-headed windows, sometimes single, sometimes grouped in threes with similar-headed doorways, that provide access to different areas of the school building *(fig. 119)*. Differing levels in the buildings echo the alternating projections and recession of the various blocks, while tall cut-stone chimneystacks add interest to the roofline. Overall, this fine building demonstrates local expertise in stone-carving and general handling of materials. A picturesque, single-storey, stone building standing on The Green at Geashill was designed to house a school by the architect John Townshend Trench (1834-1909) in 1862 *(fig. 120)*. It has a bellcote, twin stone chimneystacks with decorative terracotta ridge-cresting and fleur-de-lis finials. This important, small building has been carefully maintained and is now in use as a community centre. In the same year a much larger school and convent complex, St Brigid's Convent of Mercy, was built in Clara. A variety of window forms break the monotony on all of the elevations and a carved stone aedicule housing a statue of St Brigid at first-floor level adds emphasis to the principal façade of this austerely plain building. At St Stanislaus Roman Catholic College at Tullybeg additional buildings were added on the site during the years 1855-61 and later in 1865-70. These buildings were larger and more elaborately finished than the original plain structure; they may perhaps be seen as a measure of the growing confidence of the now well-established Roman Catholic clergy.

The middle years of the nineteenth century saw some return of prosperity to urban areas, and a number of shopfronts in the county date from this time. A simple example, Lyons of Main Street, Banagher, dating from around 1840, is typical of a form that remained popular throughout the century *(fig. 121)*. Executed in stucco, the fluted pilasters, console brackets and raised lettering on the fascia of these classic examples continued to be copied in wood in the later years of the twentieth century and was used to replace the many original shopfronts that were being swept away. In Clara, Daly's shopfront on Main Street (c. 1850) follows a simpler pattern, with narrow pilasters supporting the fascia. However, the double wooden doors with rectangular light overhead and wide windows with protective bars were popular all over the country *(fig. 122)*. An even simpler type of shopfront is used at Luker's shop in Shannonbridge (c. 1860) *(fig. 123)*. Here many of the original features have been retained, including the windows and ceramic lettering on the fascia board. No attempt has been made to ornament any of the details, although some elements have been replaced. Another house and shop in Clara, that merits description is Carey's on Main Street, where the façade has retained many original features. On the upper storeys, moulded-render surrounds emphasise the simple sash-windows and the door to the residence. Moulded quoins emphasise the corners of the building and the shopfront has handsome consoles flanking the fascia while supporting the cornice. This type of building, with residence above grocery shop/bar, was also prevalent throughout the country.

(fig. 121)
S. LYONS
Main Street
Banagher
(c. 1840)

A well preserved shopfront where the various elements are executed in cement render.

(fig. 122)
THOMAS DALY
Main Street
Clara
(c. 1850)

An example of a double shopfront with accommodation over and a separate entrance to house.

(fig. 123)
LUKER
Shannonbridge
(c. 1860)

On this shopfront the name is executed in ceramic lettering.

(fig. 124)
FANCROFT MILL
Fancroft
(c. 1820)

The derelict façade of one of the several mills that formed this industrial complex.

A number of large ruined mill buildings dating from the first half of the nineteenth century have survived to remind us of the prominent position this type of buildings once had in the landscape of County Offaly. Some of these mills were complexes of building that often included a residence for the miller. There were six mills in the vicinity of Fancroft Mill, near Roscrea, some dating from around 1820 *(fig. 124)*. This complex would have provided employment for relatively large numbers of workers, and evidence of the prosperity that such ventures created may be seen in the handsome miller's house, built in about 1860 and set behind a high wall *(fig. 125)*. Although it is a plain house, it is well built with good proportions and retains many of its original features, such as the timber sash-windows and wide Wyatt windows on the ground-floor garden elevation. Some impressive buildings that survive from the era when flour-milling was an important industry are to be seen at Belmont and Birr. At Belmont, milling had been carried out from

(fig. 125)
FANCROFT MILLER'S
HOUSE
Fancroft
(c. 1860)

A substantial dwelling house, surrounded by a high wall, was provided for the miller and also formed part of the mill complex.

the middle of the eighteenth century. The main building there, which is on an L-shaped plan, was built in 1769, altered in 1867/68 and has the following inscription 'Erected by John Clifford, Mill Wright, 1769, Gilbert Holmes and Thomas L'Estrange Esquires May Ye 21'. A later building on the site has cast-iron windows of casement design *(fig. 126)*. Another five-storey mill, at Birr, has wooden casements with yellow brick surrounds. In various locations old, tall mill and distillery buildings still survive, with their looming gaunt silhouettes serving as reminders of a lost industrial age in the county. An industrial building dating to c. 1870, in use as a bank since 1977, demonstrates the vagaries of commerce: an established business in impressive premises, in this case Goodbodys,

Agricultural Supplier, succumbed to change and after a century was taken over by a more successful commercial interest in need of a new branch office *(fig. 127)*. It is an ornate, three-storey brick building in Ruskinian Gothic, which has polychrome brick and cut-stone details, situated next door to the stone market-house in O'Connor Square in Tullamore, where it provides an interesting contrast of styles. This is an attractive building with a variety of window styles and brick detailing creating a pleasing horizontal rhythm across the façade. Vertical emphasis is provided by a single bay that has doors on each floor and a tall pointed gable with highly-decorated wooden barge-boards.

(fig. 126)
BELMONT MILLS
Bellmount
(1769 and 1867-8)

This building was formerly a flour mill granary. The projecting hoist bay is a striking feature. The mill was refurbished in the 1920s.

(fig. 127)
BANK OF IRELAND
O'Connor Square
Tullamore
(c. 1870)

Formerly Goodbodys, Agricultural Suppliers, this ornate brick building also has a projecting hoist bay, in this case it is topped by carved wooden decoration on the pointed gable.

(figs. 128-129)
BALLYNACARD HOUSE
Ballynacard
(1854)

A large house built for a member of the emerging professional classes, which is of particular interest because it has machine-tooled limestone decoration.

Despite the losses suffered following the Famine, there seems to have been plenty of money remaining in the Offaly economy. This was generated by industrial projects rather than from land-ownership and facilitated the building of substantial new houses in the county during the next decades. Many of these were built for professionals who were now in a position to have large houses built in the countryside. One such house was Ballynacard House built in 1854 for the Maxwell family, who had been engineers involved in the building of the railway network *(figs. 128-129)*. It is not a grand house but it is interesting because of the use of machine-tooled limestone decoration for the rather disproportionate consoles that support a mean cornice over the principal entrance. This is an interesting case of a technocrat applying the newest technology to a personal project. The architect John Skipton Mulvany (1813-70) was commissioned to build several houses by members of the Goodbody family, who had obtained their wealth from a variety of industrial projects ranging from cotton and linen-weaving to the manufacture of tobacco.

(fig. 130)
INCHMORE HOUSE
Kilcoursey
Clara
(c. 1860)

Designed for the Goodbody family by the architect John Skipton Mulvany. Several features such as the heavy stone portico, curved, rusticated bay with balcony and roof with wide eaves, are typical of this architect's style.

(fig. 131)
BUNREVAN HOUSE
Bunrevan
(c. 1860)

A plain house which has some details that are reminiscent of J. S. Mulvany's style.

(fig. 132)
CHARLESTOWN HOUSE
Kilbeggan Road
Clara
(c. 1790)

This house was remodelled by J. S. Mulvany who added curved bays and made other alterations to the earlier house.

(fig. 133)
ANNAGHMORE HOUSE
Annaghmore
(c. 1790)

The curved full-height bays added to this house were fashionable during the Regency period.

(fig. 134)
ANNAGHMORE HOUSE

Annaghmore's interior has a fine neo-classical bifurcating staircase.

Inchmore House was built for the family in the town of Clara. This house has had many additions and alterations made to it over the years but the two-storey façade with columned portico, wide eaves with brackets and bows to gable ends are characteristic of Mulvany's abbreviated classical style *(fig. 130)*. Another house, Bunrevan House (c. 1860) is of less formal style, but has details such as the sprocketed roof that are reminiscent of Mulvany's work *(fig. 131)*. Mulvany also remodelled the plain, square Charlestown House, Clara, originally built c. 1790, by adding curved bays and other architectural features, although it has since been altered *(fig. 132)*. Another house that was remodelled by the addition of curved bays is the unusual Annaghmore House, also c. 1790 *(figs. 133-134)*. Here full-height bays were added in about 1820, to either end of the principal façade. Extensive well-constructed outbuildings and servants' quarters are located to the rear of the house *(fig. 135)*. Several substantial houses, among them Ballinlough House, Heath and Bella Vista, Edenderry, that have modern design features, though incorporating details from an earlier period, were also being built during the later years of the nineteenth century *(figs. 136-138)*.

(fig. 135)
ANNAGHMORE HOUSE

A view of the handsome range of outbuildings. The bellcote over the entrance gate is typical for the period.

97

(fig. 136)
BALLINLOUGH HOUSE
Heath
(c. 1860)

The stucco window heads with label mouldings to first floor windows are an attractive feature of this house.

(fig. 137)
BELLA VISTA
St Mary's Road
Edenderry
(1873)

This house combines classical proportions and a modest round-headed doorway flanked by engaged Tuscan columns supporting an entablature, with modern ornamental cast-iron brackets and ridge cresting with finials.

(fig. 138)
BELLA VISTA

Detail showing cast-iron brackets.

A more unusual use of modern materials may be seen in the small corrugated-iron schoolhouse with sprocketed roof of about 1880, situated in the grounds of Beechmount House, Clara *(fig. 139)*. It was built as a school-room for the children of the Goodbody family. By contrast, a house at Drumbane, Crinkill, built c. 1880, combines features that could be said to be old fashioned, both in shape and details, for this late date *(figs. 140-141)*. It follows the familiar pattern of broad centrally placed segmental-headed doorway, flanked by engaged columns and sidelights, and has a decorative fanlight over. However, as has already been pointed out, this particular type of doorway has retained its popularity to the present day, and examples of it may be seen all over Offaly and elsewhere in the country. The centrally placed tripartite window and small flanking gabled pavilions of Crinkill hark back to the eighteenth century in an understated way.

(fig. 139)
BEECHMOUNT HOUSE
Kilbeggan Road
Clara
(c. 1880)

An unusual small school building constructed in corrugated-iron for use by children of the Goodbody family.

(figs. 140-141)
PROSPECT HOUSE
Riverstown Road
Crinkill
(c. 1880)

The principal façade of this house combines architectural elements in several styles.

Owners of the various large estates in the county constructed estate cottages for their employees. Some of these buildings were on the estates themselves, while others were sited in towns close by. Two well-designed examples situated on the Charleville estate were built to house the head gardener and gamekeeper respectively. The head gardener's house, built in 1864, has yellow brick walls with corners, window-surrounds and geometric designs elegantly executed in red brick *(fig. 142)*. Carved bargeboards and a catslide slate roof complete the decorative features of this architecturally notable house. Also executed in brick, the gamekeeper's house (1874) has polychrome brick details over the narrow sash-windows *(fig. 143)*. Projecting bay windows enliven two of the elevations. It has steep gables to the roof and these have decorated bargeboards. In Birr, some estate-workers' cottages were built at Eden Row. These cottages, for the Birr Castle Estate, won a Royal Agricultural Society Medal for their design in the 1870s. Originally all of the cottages had roughcast render to conceal the coursed-rubble limestone walls. They are of relatively generous proportions and have simple decorative features in the oculus and ornate bargeboards on the dormer and porch. A pair of former estate cottages built in Geashill in about 1860 are well finished, with attractive details in the carved stone lintels over the doors and windows, yellow brick chimneys and stone gate piers that all add character to these small buildings *(figs. 144-145)*. Also in Geashill is a good example of the blacksmith's forge, c. 1870, which was a feature of most towns and villages in the country. Here the whole ensemble of forge, with a particularly well-carved horseshoe-shaped doorway, outbuildings, pump and yard, has survived in good order *(fig. 146)*.

(fig. 142)
HEAD GARDENER'S HOUSE
Charleville Castle Demesne
(1864)

A well designed house with simple lines, which has finely executed brickwork.

(fig. 143)
GAME KEEPER'S HOUSE
Charleville Castle Demesne
(1874)

A variety of window types, steeply pitched roof and quality of the brick detailing make this an oustanding example of estate architecture.

(fig. 144)
ESTATE COTTAGES
Dalgan
Geashill
(c. 1860)

These small stone-built estate cottages set behind low stone walls have tall chimneys and an attractive form of latticed window.

(fig. 145)
ESTATE COTTAGES

A view showing the unusual detailing in the carved stone lintels.

(fig. 146)
CURRAGH
Geashill
(c. 1870)

This forge forms part of a surviving group of building, which includes outbuildings, pump and yard.

(fig. 147)
**CLARA QUAKER
MEETING HOUSE**
Frederick Street
Clara
(1867)

A modest classical pediment crowns the principal façade of the Quaker meeting house in Clara.

(fig. 148)
**TULLAMORE
PRESBYTERIAN CHURCH**
High Street
Tullamore
(c. 1865)

A severely classical building featuring an interesting juxtaposition of two pediments.

The large Quaker community in the county had prospered over the centuries and they had a new meeting-house at Frederick Street in Clara designed by John Skipton Mulvany. It is an Italianate building of about 1850, single-storey with a stone ashlar façade and stylish features. There is a projecting temple front topped with a pediment, and flanking bays that have windows with Y-tracery; the corners are finished with carved quoins *(fig. 147)*. A more severely classical building is the Presbyterian church on High Street, Tullamore of c. 1865. Built at a cost of £300 on a T-shaped plan, the porch and main block have echoing pediments with plain entablature supported on pilasters. A distinguished building set behind low wall and rail-

(fig. 149)
BIRR TOWN LIBRARY
John's Place
Birr
(1885)

Formerly a Presbyterian church, built in a pared down Gothic Revival style.

(fig. 150)
ST BRIGID'S
CATHOLIC CHURCH
Bridge Street/
The Square
Clara
(1881)

A large church built in
the Gothic Revival style,
designed by the architect
J. J. O'Callaghan. The
spire was added in the
1930s.

(fig. 151)
ST BRIGID'S
CATHOLIC CHURCH

Detail of a naturalistic
carved stone flower from
a doorway.

(fig. 152)
ST BRIGID'S
CATHOLIC CHURCH

ings, on an important site in the town, this church is an asset to the town's architectural heritage *(fig. 148)*. Although there is a contrast in styles between the neo-classicism of the Tullamore church and the neo-Gothicism used in the former Presbyterian church, at John's Place, Birr (c. 1885) they are both executed in an austere manner. The tall twin lancet windows on the façade of the Birr church have a distinctive schematic form of the rose window, and while there are several other features using the Gothic vocabulary, these are rendered very plainly *(fig. 149)*. Larger, more elaborate and with Gothic motifs used in a more traditional manner, is St Brigid's Roman Catholic church, The Square, Clara. The building was designed in 1876 by the architect John Joseph O'Callaghan (c. 1838-1905) and completed in 1881, with the spire added in 1930 *(figs. 150-152)*. It dominates an important corner site in the centre of the town. Also dating to 1881 is St Columba's Church of Ireland church in

(fig. 153)
**ST COLUMBA'S
CHURCH
Aghancarnan
(1881)**

An unusual Gothic Revival
church which has strongly
individualistic design features. The east end has a
steeply pitched roofline
rising up to a tall, but-
tressed belfry.

(fig. 154)
**ST COLUMBA'S
CHURCH**

A detail of the side elevation showing triple lancet
windows and repeated
use of buttressing on
porch and other features.

(fig. 155)
BIRR THEATRE AND ARTS CENTRE
Oxmantown Mall
Birr
(1888)

Originally the parish hall, this building in the Tudor Revival style has many finely carved decorative features on its façade. It is an outstanding example of a building influenced by the Arts and Crafts movement.

(fig. 156)
BIRR THEATRE AND ARTS CENTRE

Decorative detail from the principal façade, showing a carved heraldic lion holding a shield.

Aghancarnan. Constructed in heavily rusticated limestone, it has an unusual bellcote with a spire situated above the entrance porch *(figs. 153-154)*. Although it is no longer in use as a church, it has been carefully conserved and retains many original features including stained-glass windows.

A number of fine new buildings linked to the existing Church of Ireland church were erected during the 1880s and 1890s along the broad Oxmantown Mall in Birr. The most important of these was the former parish hall, the design of which was influenced by the Arts and Crafts movement. Here elements of Historicism in the Tudor Revival style were combined with carefully carved details, often in wood *(figs. 155-156)*. It was designed by the architect J. Franklin Fuller (1835-1924) and built in the late 1880s; it stands back from the tree-lined road, set behind cast-iron gates and tall railings. A modest house on Oxmantown Mall, built as the sexton's house c. 1880, also shows the influence of the Arts and Crafts movement with some Tudor style timbering; other decorative details include a stained-glass oculus on the east elevation, pan-tiled roof and cresting on the roof ridge. St Brendan's Church of Ireland church was extended and embel-

ST BRENDAN'S CHURCH

Detail of decoration on the wooden louver.

(fig. 157)
ST BRENDAN'S CHURCH
Oxmantown Mall
Birr
(1815)

A plain building where applied Gothic motifs such as the crocketed finials sit awkwardly with the castellations on the principal façade. Many additions and alterations were made to this large Church of Ireland church during the later nineteenth century.

(fig. 158)
ST BRENDAN'S CHURCH

The interior of this church is a more successful architectural composition in the Gothic manner than the exterior.

ST BRENDAN'S
CHURCH
Oxmantown Mall
Birr

This sketch shows a
drawing for the reredos
dated to the 9th
December 1885 that
had been agreed by
the Select Vestry.

ST BRENDAN'S
CHURCH
Oxmantown Mall
Birr

This letter and specifica-
tion shows further addi-
tions for the new reredos
and dates to the 3rd
October 1904.

lished in two phases of alterations carried out there during the 1870s and 1890s *(fig. 157)*. This fine Gothic Revival building had a new chancel designed by the architect Thomas Drew (1838-1910) added in 1876, and a splendid east window was commissioned from Charles Kempe by the fourth Earl of Rosse in 1891 *(fig. 158)*. Other additions made at this time included a decorative reredos that caused some controversy because of its inclusion of religious images. This important building closes the vista down Oxmantown Mall from the entrance gates of Birr Castle and forms yet another architecturally pleasing element in the town.

A monument to the Manchester Martyrs in Market Square, Birr was erected in 1894. It takes the form of the figure of the Maid of Erin flanked by the symbolic harp and wolfhound, standing on a low column, which in turn stands on a pedestal. Situated on a prominent site at the opposite end of Main Street, it provides an architectural counterpoint to the column in Emmet Square.

There was an upsurge of bank building during the later part of the century. At that time banks were having large buildings usually classical in style, constructed in many towns around the country. Recently, changing trends within the banking system has meant that many of these impressive buildings are now being used for other purposes. One such bank building, now in use by a firm of solicitors, was the former Bank of Ireland in Tullamore. Designed by Sandham Symes in 1879, the Italianate façade has finely carved stone details, particularly on the keystone over the entrance door and on the console brackets and cornice of the upper storey. The building stands behind cast-iron railings and is a handsome addition to High Street *(figs. 159-162)*. A custom-built bank building is situated on JKL Street, Edenderry. Here it will be seen that all of the emphasis is on the ground floor, where business was carried out, while accommodation was provided in the upper storeys. The tall two-bay entrance is marked by pilasters flanking the round-headed doorway; this is supported on columns, with an ornate keystone containing a fruit swag with the letters HBL making reference to its former owners, the Hibernian Bank Limited *(figs. 163-164)*.

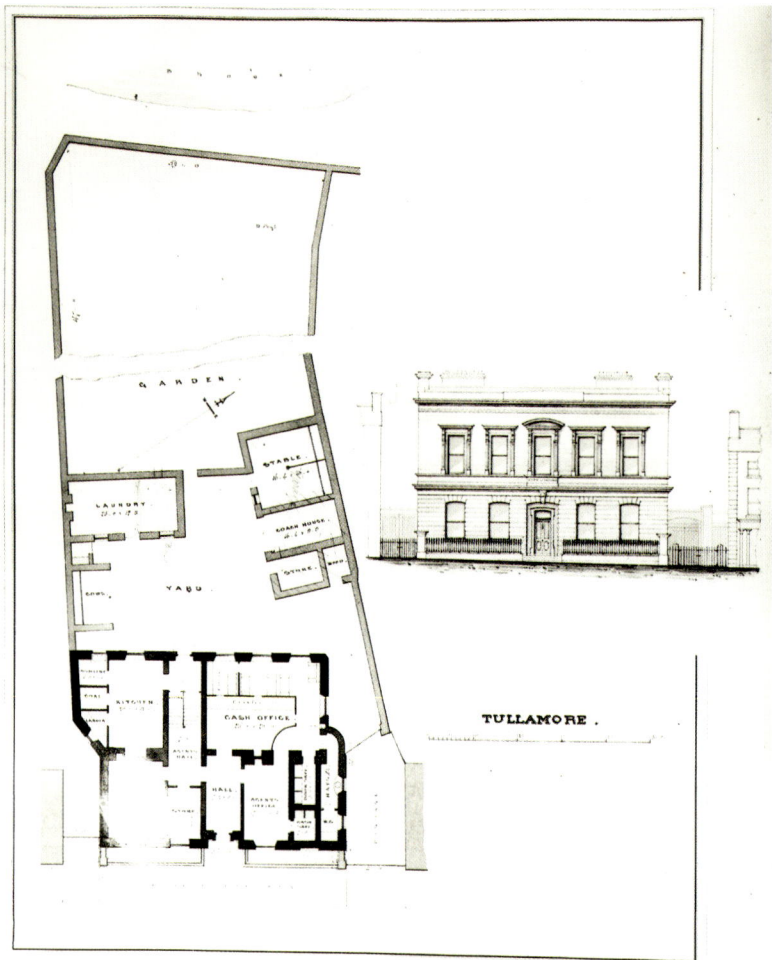

TULLAMORE.

(fig. 159)
HOEY AND DENNING
High Street
Tullamore
(c. 1879)

Survey of the plan and front elevation, c. 1879, of the former bank in High Street Tullamore by the architect Sandham Symes.

Courtesy of the Irish Architectural Archive.

(fig. 160)
HOEY AND DENNING

(fig. 161)
HOEY AND DENNING

A detail of the crisply carved dentils on the cornice of the building.

(fig. 162)
HOEY AND DENNING

A detail of the ornate supporting brackets on the windows on the upper floor.

(fig. 163)
BANK OF IRELAND
JKL Street
Edenderry
(c. 1890)

A later bank building where emphasis is all on the ground floor, which housed the banking hall. The upper storey is plain except for a decorated cornice, horizontal string course and pilasters that are used to continue the vertical lines of the entrance door.

(fig. 164)
BANK OF IRELAND

Detail of the carved keystone bearing the initials HBL for Hibernian Bank Limited.

The Twentieth Century

During the early years of the twentieth century Ireland enjoyed a period of comparative peace, and during that time several small-scale public buildings, such as dispensaries, post offices and new police barracks, were constructed around the county. A former dispensary building in Daingean built in about 1900 is a typical example. Built of snecked limestone with red brick features and trim, it is unusual in that its quoins are executed in the brick rather than vice versa, which is far more common *(fig. 165)*. In Kinnitty, a former RIC barracks (c. 1900), now used as a Garda station, retains many of its original features, such as the tripartite windows on the lower storey and original six-over-six glazing pattern in the windows on the floor above *(fig. 166)*. Round-headed openings are used for the carriageway, entrance doors and central window of the ground floor and these provide a pleasing rhythm. The post office in Emmet Square, Birr (1903) shows the influence of the Arts and Crafts movement in its historical architectural references, where volutes and segmental pediment are perched on the tall gable and in its variety of window styles *(figs. 167-168)*. A handsome limestone canopy with glazed fanlight and part-glazed double doors beneath marks the entrance. This well-designed building shows careful attention to detail. Tullamore post office in O'Connor Square (1909) features a similar stone canopy over the entrance doorway, which is combined with a limestone ashlar doorcase and spider-web fanlight *(figs. 169-170)*. The roughcast render on this building tends to disguise the vertical emphasis.

(fig. 165)
MOLESWORTH STREET
Daingean
(c. 1900)

A former dispensary building with matching, substantial doctor's residence to one side.

(fig. 166)
GARDA STATION
KINNITTY
(c. 1900)

A six-bay former RIC barracks where various doors, windows and a carriage arch form a pleasing rhythm on the principal façade.

JKL STREET
Edenderry
(c. 1905)

This pillar box was manufactured by the Leeds firm of founders Andrew Handyside & Co. who were in operation from c. 1853-1933.

(fig. 167)
BIRR POST OFFICE
Emmet Square
(1903)

An impressive post office building, built in a style influenced by the Arts and Crafts movement. Many different decorative elements are combined on the front elevation.

(fig. 168)
BIRR POST OFFICE

A detail of the handsome limestone canopy supported on brackets and original part glazed door.

(fig. 169)
TULLAMORE POST OFFICE
O'Carroll Square
Tullamore
(1909)

This custom-built post office building has a similar curved canopy but a very different style of roof.

(fig. 170)
TULLAMORE POST OFFICE

In this example the limestone canopy is supported on paired brackets.

R.J. BARBER
Main Street
Birr
(c. 1900)

One of the best surviving shopfronts from this period in County Offaly is that of R.J. Barber. Winner of the Traditional Shopfront National Award in 1978.

R.J. BARBER

It has elaborately carved consoles and a cornice decorated with the classically inspired egg and dart or ovolo moulding. The painted lettering is an example of the 'shadowed' type, which creates a three-dimensional effect.

KINNITTY
(c. 1900)

A pair of distinctive houses in Kinnitty. The narrow paired sash windows have decorative details and round heads are set in segmental arched openings with keystones above. The same form of arch and keystone is used for the doorways which have timber battened 'half-doors'. Unusual two-tiered chimneystacks are panelled and rendered.

Also during these years efforts were being made to improve housing conditions, and local authorities were involved in building schemes to house people who had lived in the ubiquitous lanes that were a feature of so many midland towns. One such scheme was at Convent View Terrace, in Tullamore in about 1900, where the attractive terraced houses have a variety of windows and brick details on rendered walls that enliven the façades of these small buildings *(fig. 171)*.

(fig. 171)
20-21 CONVENT VIEW TERRACE
Tullamore
(c. 1900)

The varied and irregular positioning of windows is an attractive feature of these early local authority houses.

(fig. 172)
KILLEIGH ROAD
Tullamore
(c. 1900)
A substantial red brick
suburban house, which
has handsome details,
is typical of houses that
were being built for the
professional classes in the
early years of the century.

(fig. 173)
BIRR ROAD
Tullamore
(1906)

A red brick, asymmetrical
bungalow designed by
the architect F.G. Hicks in
1906 in suburban
Tullamore.

Substantial houses for the professional classes and merchants were being built on the outskirts of towns. On Killeigh Road, Tullamore, a well-built house, constructed in red brick and tooled limestone dressing, has classically inspired motifs over the entrance *(fig. 172)*. Typical details for the period also feature; these include stained-glass inserts in all of the windows of the principal façade and in the half-glazed double entrance doors. In about 1906 the architect F. G. Hicks designed an asymmetrical spreading bungalow on the Birr Road in Tullamore *(fig. 173)*. Built of red brick and set back in its own grounds, this house has pleasing proportions and retains many of its original features.

Around the county, churches and schools were also being constructed; one of these was the small national school at Chapel Lane, Daingean. It is typical of the plain, functional buildings in general use in the country. This small building retains many of its original features, including the timber sash-windows with six-over-nine glazing pattern and the battened door. There is a bootscraper outside the door, a reminder of the times when children walked long distances on muddy roads to school. A much larger educational establishment was built in Edenderry. St Mary's Convent, St Mary's Road was built in 1916 to a design by the architect William Anthony Scott (1871-1921). This architect, while an exponent of the Arts and Crafts style, is also regarded as one of the practitioners of early modernism in Ireland *(fig. 174)*. The convent, a comparatively simple building, echoes some of the design features of the nearby St Mary's Roman Catholic church, built 1916, by the same architect. In the

(fig. 175)
**ST MARY'S
CATHOLIC CHURCH
St Mary's Road
Edenderry
(1916)**

W.A. Scott also designed this large church. As a leading architect of the Celtic Revival he is well known for his free intrerpretation of the Hiberno Romanesque style.

(fig. 176)
**ST MARY'S
CATHOLIC CHURCH**

The interior showing the use of well-spaced round arches reminiscent of the Romanesque style combined with classical Diocletian windows.

church, strong verticals and wide round-headed doorways combine with a schematic rendering of the Hiberno-Romanesque style to the principal entrance, which is framed by flanking buttresses *(figs. 175-176)*. Wide round arches supported on polished stone columns line the nave, and an exposed trussed roof with Diocletian windows to the clerestory, feature in the interior.

**ST MARY'S
CATHOLIC CHURCH**
Pollagh
(1909; stained glass
1930s)

Two fine stained glass
windows from the Studio
of Harry Clarke (1889-
1931) contrast with the
dark bog yew altar and
tabernacle of the church.
Depicted are the Blessed
Virgin and the Sacred
Heart. The juxtaposition of
the blue gown worn by
the Virgin and the con-
trasting red robes of the
Sacred Heart is subtly
articulated through the
interplay of variants on
the colour scheme within
the design.

(fig. 177)
THE BRIDGE HOUSE
Bridge Street
Tullamore
(c. 1910)

Designed by the architect
T.F. McNamara, the principal façade of the Bridge
House retains many of its
original features and is a
splendid example of its
type.

(fig. 178)
THE BRIDGE HOUSE

A detail of a finely carved
keystone from the ground
floor.

The building of large shops with elaborate façades may be seen as indicators of the growing prosperity of Tullamore during the early decades of the twentieth century. One of these, The Bridge House, originally built for P & H Egan in 1910 by the architect T.F. McNamara, still retains many details of its original façade *(figs. 177-178)*. The second example, designed by the same architect, was built as a drapery store for Malachy Scally during the years 1911-14 *(figs. 179-180)*. In the 1970s the splendid curved display-windows were removed, but many interesting architectural features have survived, such as the eccentric capitals on the ground floor and the decorative roofline with balustrade, central gable and finials.

By the 1920s modernism as an architectural style had been introduced into Ireland and in the following decade, when new hospitals were being built around the country, all were modern in style. Tullamore Hospital, built between 1937 and 1942, was designed by the architectural practice of Michael Scott (1905-89) and Norman Good. This building was constructed using traditional rugged limestone masonry, but the combination of strong design features, window variety, large glazed areas and curved central bay all point to the influence of modern Dutch architecture.

(fig. 179)
SCALLY'S
Columcille Street
Tullamore
(1911-14)

Malachy Scally's was one
of the finest premises in
Tullamore. The well-exe-
cuted stone dressings,
particularly the urns
and capitals, compare
favourably with similar
decoration on the Bridge
House.

*Courtesy of the National
Library of Ireland.*

(fig. 180)
SCALLY'S
Columcille Street
Tullamore
(1911-14)

A detail of the capitals on
the ground floor.

Most of Offaly remained quietly rural in the decades after the Second World War. Only a small number of buildings of any distinction can be dated to this period. The Allied Irish Bank, on Columcille Street, Tullamore (1949) was designed by the architect J. R. Boyd-Barrett. This building has deceptively simple lines and quality design features, such as the brass-framed window, the finely dressed stone, tall narrow windows above and glazed panelled doors. Boyd-Barrett had earlier been involved in such ground-breaking buildings as the headquarters of the then Department of Industry and Commerce, Kildare Street (1935-8), and in the supervision of the construction of the revolutionary Church of Christ the King, Cork, for the Chicago architect Barry Byrne.

Although there had been many proposals for projects to utilise the resources of Offaly's extensive bogs over the centuries, it was not until the Turf Development Act 1950 provided for the building of houses for workers employed there that any real architectural impact was made on the landscape of the county. Two of these schemes were built at Bracknagh for the Clonsast Works and Kilcormac for Boora Works, while a third, at Rochfortbridge in County Westmeath, was constructed to house workers

(fig. 182)
ESB SUBSTATION
Glebe Street
Birr
(1949)

A detail showing the distinctive thunderbolt and wave motif in use by the ESB at that time.

(fig. 181)
ESB POWER STATION
Rhode
(1956-63)

Cooling towers were an outstanding feature of the Offaly landscape. This view of the peat-fired generating station at Rhode shows the construction of these towers. There was no large natural supply of water in the Rhode area, so it was necessary to use a re-circulating system for cooling water to cool the condensers.

Courtesy of the National Library of Ireland.

from the Derrygreenagh Works in County Offaly. These housing schemes were designed by Frank Gibney (1905-78) and contained a number of types that provided simple but modern accommodation. Gibney's ideas are derived from various sources, including the English Garden City movement and 1930s architecture in the Netherlands. His distinctive style involves the use of enclosure, coherent design and varied building types within the schemes. Several industrial-type structures associated with bog workings had been erected during the late nineteenth century, but it was not until the advent of large-scale briquette factories, and the use of milled peat for the power stations of the Electricity Supply Board during the 1950s, that some architecturally important buildings were constructed. The German firm of Buckau Wolf

(fig. 183)
MARY MOTHER OF GOD CATHOLIC CHURCH
Chapel Lane
Daingean
(1960)

A fine example of modern church design by the architect J.R. Boyd-Barrett.

designed the briquette factory at Croghan that went into production in 1961 and the office buildings nearby. These structures are of the modest scale and modern design typical of the period. The entrance gates have unusual and striking gateposts. Three large power stations utilising milled peat were built at Ferbane, Rhode and Shannonbridge. These were huge construction projects; the earliest was begun at Ferbane in 1953 and additions were made to all three sites over the years. The enormous cooling-towers were the most distinctive features on the landscape for half a century and could be seen for miles across the flat countryside *(fig. 181)*. All three power stations have been superseded by new technology and are being replaced by the West Offaly Power Plant. More notable for a design feature than as a building,

the little Electricity Supply Board station in Glebe Street, Birr (1949), has a dated plaque with distinctive thunderbolt and wave motif *(fig. 182)*.

Other notable buildings from the second half of the twentieth century include the Church of Mary Mother of God in Daingean, built in 1960 to a design by J.R. Boyd-Barrett. Here traditional features, such as the centrally placed spire, the large west window with the statue of the Virgin Mary below, are combined with modern materials and design *(fig. 183)*. It was constructed at a cost of £60,000 by Turley Builders of Portarlington. The design of the interior, which has dramatic concrete ribs of varied shapes, light painted walls and colourful modern stained glass, is striking *(figs. 184-185)*.

(fig. 184)
MARY MOTHER OF GOD CATHOLIC CHURCH

This view of the interior shows the striking pattern made by concrete ribs used to support the roof.

Changes were being introduced into the educational system, and Birr was chosen as the site for a large community school during the 1970s, when there was an architectural competition for the design of a prototypical community school. Designed by the practice of Peter & Mary Doyle, it was constructed using modern materials and built in 1976-9. Ultimately derived from industrial building systems, the school offered a pleasant and open environment.

As the twentieth century moved to a close, Offaly, like many other rural counties in Ireland, began to experience growth and expansion in the towns, resulting in the construction of many new buildings and extensive housing estates. There are also some impressive public buildings of this period; among these, the County Hall in Tullamore is a fine example, designed by the architectural practice of Ahrens, Burton & Koralek. Conceived as a timber-clad pavilion, the building was set in a mature Victorian garden on the edge of the town. Natural materials were used where possible in the construction of the building and efforts were made to retain the mature trees that occupied the site.

(fig. 185)
MARY MOTHER OF GOD CATHOLIC CHURCH
Chapel Lane
Daingean
(1960)

This striking depiction of the Virgin with attendant angels provides a dramatic focus to the west end of the church.

Conclusion

Ireland's increasing prosperity, particularly in the last decade, has seen major changes in both urban and rural areas. Counties close to Dublin are under particular pressure as the growing population of the city spreads further and further outside its boundaries. Small urban settlements are being overwhelmed by estates that sometimes house greater numbers than the entire population of the original village. Most noticeable is the loss of original shopfronts, particularly in busy towns where few, if any, pre-1980 examples remain. Often a simple nineteenth-century upper floor sits uncomfortably and unnoticed above a modernised ground-floor façade.

Nevertheless, some small villages and towns, such as Geashill, Cloghan, Kinnitty, Banagher and Shannonbridge, have retained much of their original architectural fabric. Some exemplary local restoration projects, such as the Crank House in Banagher, have also been carried out. Of the larger towns, Birr, designated a heritage town, is the most impressive and retains a generous range of quality urban buildings dating back to the early eighteenth century. Churches, shopfronts, terraces of fine hous-

es, church halls, schools, convents, all share a setting of inspired, if limited, town planning that had elegant malls, squares and vistas laid out in a coherent fashion. Particularly striking is the retention of so many of the small original features, such as windows, railings, walls, street-furniture and gardens, that have been lost in so many other towns in the county.

An understanding of the context of our architectural heritage serves to enrich the experience of those who encounter it. Who could fail to be impressed by such examples as the dramatic siting of the stags' heads on the gate pillars that mark the entrance to the Castropetre Church of Ireland church in Edenderry, or the painstaking brickwork of the houses on the Charleville estate, or even the elegant yet functional arches of the many canal bridges in the county?

And while it is useful to look back in order to appreciate the past, it is essential to plan for the future. The recently built 'green' County Hall in Tullamore may be seen to provide both an example and a hub for the future development of County Offaly.

Further Reading

Aalen, F.H.A., Kevin Whelan, and Matthew Stout, eds., *Atlas of the Irish Rural Landscape* (Cork, 1997).

Becker, Annette, John Olley, and Wilfried Wang, eds, *20th-Century Architecture Ireland* (Munich, 1997).

Bence-Jones, Mark, Burkes's *Guide to Country Houses, vol. 1, Ireland* (New York, 1978).

Byrne, Michael, *A Walk Through Tullamore* (Tullamore, 1980).

Cooke, Thomas Lalor, *The Early History of the Town of Birr or Parsonstown* (Reprint Tullamore, 1990).

Craig, Maurice, *'The Quest for Sir Edward Lovett Pearce', Irish Arts Review Yearbook, 1996, vol. 12* (Dublin, 1995).

Craig, Maurice, and The Knight of Glin, *Ireland Observed* (Cork, 1970).

Craig, Maurice, *Classic Irish Houses of the Middle Size* (London, 1976).

Craig, Maurice, *The Architecture of Ireland from earliest times to 1880* (London, 1989).

Delaney, Brendan, Peter Carroll, and Judith Doherty, eds., *A Heritage Inventory of ESB Buildings in Ireland* (Dublin, 2005).

Feehan, John, and Alison Rosse, *An Atlas of Birr* (Dublin, 2005).

Foster, Roy, ed., *The Oxford Illustrated History of Ireland* (London,1991).

Hood, Susan, *'Documentary Evidence for the Irish Planned Town - A Case Study of Birr', in The Town - Conservation in the Urban Area, Conference Proceedings, ed., Jane Fenlon* (Dublin, 1995).

Howley, James, *The Follies and Garden Buildings of Ireland* (New Haven and London, 1993).

Kerrigan, Paul, *Castles and Fortifications in Ireland 1485-1945* (Cork, 1995).

Laffan, William, *'From Paper to Pillar, Miscelanea Structura Curiosa and the Cumberland Column', in Miscelanea Structura Curiosa by Samuel Chearnley, ed., William Laffan* (Tralee, 2005).

Leask, H.G., *Irish Castles* (Dundalk, 1973).

Manning, Conleth, *Clonmacnoise* (Cork, 1994).

Nolan, William, and Timothy P. O'Neill, *Offaly History & Society* (Dublin, 1998).

O'Brien, Caimin, and P. David Sweetman, *Archaeological Inventory of County Offaly* (Dublin, 1997).

O'Reilly, Barry, *Living Under Thatch Vernacular Architecture in Co. Offaly* (Cork, 2004).

Rosse, The Countess of, *'Plasterwork Restotation at Birr Castle', in Irish Arts Review Yearbook, 1991-1992, pp.214-217.*

Rothery, Sean, *A Field Guide to the Building of Ireland* (Dublin, 1997).

Rothery, Sean, *Ireland and the New Architecture* (Dublin, 1997).

Scott, Michael, ed., *Hall's Ireland, Mr & Mrs Hall's Tour of 1840* (London, 1984).

Swift, Michael, *Historical Maps of Ireland* (London, 1999).

Williams, Jeremy, *A Companion Guide to Architecture in Ireland, 1837-1921* (Dublin, 1994).

Wright, John, *Offaly One Hundred Years Ago* (Reprint Tullamore, 1989).

Registration Numbers

The structures mentioned in the text of this Introduction are listed below. It is possible to find more information on each structure by accessing our survey on the Internet at: **www.buildingsofireland.ie** *and searching by the Registration Number. Structures are listed by page number.*

09 Clonmacnoise
Not included in survey.

09 Durrow
Not included in survey.

09 Castlefield Bridge, Cadamstown
Not included in survey.

10 Ballycowan Fortified House,
Ballycowan
Not included in survey.

10 Knockarley House, Knockarley
Reg. 14939016

11 Clonony Towerhouse, Clonony
Not included in survey.

11 Leap Castle, Leap
Reg. 14939007

11 Emmel Castle, Emmel West
Reg. 14944013

11 Ballycumber House,
Ballycumber
Reg. 14801010

11 Killeigh House, Killeigh
Reg. 14813002

11 Ballyshiel House
Not included in survey.

12 Former Barracks, Main Street,
Banagher
Reg. 14810033

12 Syngefield House, Clonoghil
Upper, Birr
Reg. 14935005

12 Gloster House, Glasderry More
Reg. 14942015

14 Gloster Obelisk, Glasderry More
Reg. 14942016

14 Arch Hall, Wilkinstown,
Co. Meath
Not included in survey.

14 Stillorgan House, Co. Dublin
Not included in survey.

16 Emmel Castle, Emmel West
Reg. 14944013

16 Leap Castle, Leap
Reg. 14939007

17 Bridge House, Bridge Street,
Tullamore
Reg. 14807013

18 Round House, High Street,
Tullamore
Reg. 14807031

18 Crank House Visitor Centre,
Main Street, Banagher
Reg. 14810020

18 Balliver House, Balliver
Reg. 14922009

20 Milltown Park House, Milltown
(Cl. By.)
Reg. 14942007

20 Stables, Milltown Park House,
Milltown (Cl. By.)
Reg. 14942033

21 Springfield House, Ballyhugh or
Springfield
Reg. 14919002

21 Cumberland Column, Emmet
Square, Birr
Reg. 14819004

22 Dooly's Hotel, Emmet Square,
Birr
Reg. 14819009

22 Cumberland House, Emmet
Square, Birr
Reg. 14819001

22 Windmill, Ballystrig
Reg. 14911014

25 Belmont Bridge, Belmont
Reg. 14824009

25 Millgrove Bridge,
Millgrove/Nahana
Reg. 14927004

24 Portnahinch Bridge,
Garryhinch
Reg. 14933010

25 Blundell Aqueduct,
Edenderry/Drumcooly/
Cloncannon
Reg. 14912008

26 Downshire Bridge, Edenderry
Reg. 14912005

27 Canal Warehouse, Main Street,
Daingean
Reg. 14808023

27 Bury Bridge, Convent Road,
Tullamore
Reg. 14807089

28 The Canal Hotel, Shannon
Harbour
Reg. 14922005

28 Harbour Master's House,
Shannon Harbour
Reg. 14922006

28 Dry Docks, Shannon Harbour
Reg. 14922014

28 Lock-keeper's House,
Shannonbridge
Reg. 14805008

29 Boland's Lock-keeper's House,
Cappancur
Reg. 14917019

29 Victoria Lock, Clonahenoge
Reg. 14929012

31 St Brigid's Church of Ireland
Church, Church Road, Clara
Reg. 14802050

31 SS Peter and Paul Roman
Catholic Church, Clyduff
(Cl. By.)
Reg. 14910002

31 Claremount House, Claremount
Reg. 14929002

32 The Doon, Doon Demesne
Reg. 14906002

33 Thatched House, Ballyegan
Reg. 14938015

33 Thatched House, Cloncon
Reg. 14917009

35 Thatched House, Derrinduff
Reg. 14935007

35 Thatched House, Killurin
Reg. 14925003

35 Thatched Outbuilding,
Ballyduff South
Reg. 14918014

35 Thatched Outbuilding,
Ballyduff South
Reg. 14918015

35 Thatched Outbuilding,
Ballyduff South
Reg. 14918016

35 Thatched Outbuilding,
Ballyduff South
Reg. 14918017

34 Dan and Molly's, Ballyboy
Reg. 14816004

34 Ballydownan Cottage, Geashill
Reg. 14814025

35 Limekiln, Glenregan
Reg. 14937001

36 Crinkill Barracks, Barracks
Street, Crinkill
Reg. 14820012

38 Daingean Courthouse, The
Square, Daingean
Reg. 14808007

38 Birr Courthouse, Townsend
Street, Birr
Reg. 14819055

129

86 Shannon Bridge,
Shannonbridge
Reg. 14805010

86 Banagher Bridge, Banagher
Reg. 14810034

86 Derrinsallow Bridge, Bunrevan
Reg. 14935002

87 Ballycumber Bridge,
Ballycumber/Ballybruncullin/
Bohernagrisna
Reg. 14801009

87 Kilcumber Bridge,
Kilcumber/Ballykilleen
(Cl. By.)/Ballinowlart North
Reg. 14919004

86 Geashill Railway Station, Ard
Reg. 14926001

87 Railway Station, Tullamore
Railway Station, Tullamore
Reg. 14807106, 14807107

87 Signal Box, Tullamore Railway
Station, Tullamore
Reg. 14807108

87 Footbridge, Tullamore Railway
Station, Tullamore
Reg. 14807105

87 Gaol Bridge, Charleville
Road/Cormac Street, Tullamore
Reg. 14807109

88 St. John's Convent of Mercy,
Wilmer Road, Birr
Reg. 14819188

91 Model National School, Model
School Road, Birr
Reg. 14819291

91 National School, The Green,
Geashill
Reg. 14814001

91 St. Brigid's Convent of Mercy,
Kilbeggan Road, Clara
Reg. 14802011

91 St. Stanislaus's Roman Catholic
College, Tullybeg
Reg. 14916004

92 S. Lyons, Main Street, Banagher
Reg. 14810014

92 Thomas Daly, Main Street,
Clara
Reg. 14802041

92 Luker, Shannonbridge
Reg. 14805006

92 M. Carey, Main Street, Clara
Reg. 14802045

93 Fancroft Mill, Fancroft
Reg. 14943002

93 Miller's House, Fancroft
Reg. 14943003

93 Corn and Oat Mill, Belmont
Mill, Bellmount or Lisderg
Reg. 14824006

93 Mill Granary, Belmont Mill,
Bellmount or Lisderg
Reg. 14824008

93 Mill, Newbridge Street, Birr
Reg. 14819231

94 Bank of Ireland, O'Connor
Square, Tullamore
Reg. 14807016

95 Ballynarcard House,
Ballynarcard
Reg. 14931004

97 Inchmore House, Clara
Reg. 14802018

97 Bunrevan House, Bunrevan
Reg. 14935001

97 Charlestown House, Kilbeggan
Road, Clara
Reg. 14802006

97 Annaghamore House,
Annaghmore (Ba. By.)
Reg. 14924007

97 Ballinlough House, Heath
(Cl. By.)
Reg. 14943001

97 Bella Vista, St. Mary's Road,
Edenderry
Reg. 14804044

99 School House, Beechmount
House, Kilbeggan Road, Clara
Reg. 14802013

99 House, Riverstown Road,
Crinkill
Reg. 14820005

100 Head Gardener's House,
Charleville Demesne
Reg. 14917010

100 Gamekeeper's House,
Charleville Demesne
Reg. 14917012

100 1-8 Eden Row, Birr
Reg. 14819283-14819290

100 Estate Worker's Houses,
Geashill
Reg. 14814010-14814011

100 Forge, Geashill
Reg. 14814015

102 Quaker Meeting House,
Frederick Street, Clara
Reg. 14802017

102 Presbyterian Church, High
Street, Tullamore
Reg. 14807034

103 Birr Town Library, former
Presbyterian Church, John's
Place, Birr
Reg. 14819250

103 St. Brigid's Roman Catholic
Church, Church Street/The
Square, Clara
Reg. 14802038

105 St. Columba's Church of
Ireland Church, Aghancarnan
Reg. 14909005

105 Birr Theatre and Arts Centre,
former Oxmantown Hall,
Oxmantown Mall,
Birr
Reg. 14819077

107 St. Brendan's Church of Ireland
Church, Oxmantown Mall, Birr
Reg. 14819024

108 Manchester Martyrs Memorial,
Market Square, Birr
Reg. 14819119

108 Hoey and Denning, former
Bank of Ireland, High Street,
Tullamore
Reg. 14807028

108 Bank of Ireland, JKL Street,
Edenderry
Reg. 14804026

110 Former Dispensary, Molesworth
Street, Daingean
Reg. 14808026

110 Kinnitty Garda Station,
Kinnitty
Reg. 14821011

110 Post Office, Emmet Square, Birr
Reg. 14819011

110 Post Office, O'Connor Square,
Tullamore
Reg. 14807023

111 Post Box, Edenderry
Reg. 14804036

112 R.J. Barber, Main Street, Birr
Reg. 14819154

113 Houses, Kinnitty
Reg. 14821005

113 17-21 Convent View Terrace,
Tullamore
Reg. 14807093-14807097

114 House, Killeigh Road,
Tullamore
Reg. 14807114

114 House, Birr Road, Tullamore
Reg. 14807124

115 National School, Chapel Lane,
Daingean
Reg. 14808010

115 St. Mary's Convent National
School, St. Mary's Road,
Edenderry
Reg. 14804041

115 St. Mary's Convent, St. Mary's
Road, Edenderry
Reg. 14804042

115 St. Mary's Roman Catholic
Church, St. Marys' Road,
Edenderry
Reg. 14804043

117 The Blessed Virgin and The
Sacred Heart, St. Mary's Roman
Catholic
Church, Pollagh
Reg. 14915005

118 The Bridge House, Bridge
Street, Tullamore
Reg. 14807013

118 Shopping Arcade, Columcille
Street, Tullamore
Reg. 14807004

118 Tullamore General Hospital,
Tullamore
Reg. 14917004

119 Allied Irish Bank, Columcille
Street, Tullamore
Reg. 14807005

119 Clonsast Works Housing
Scheme, Bracknagh
Not included in survey.

119 Boora Works Housing Scheme,
Kilcormac
Not included in survey.

121 Former Brickette Factory, Esker
Beg
Reg. 14918011-14918012

121 Cooling Tower, Power Station,
Rhode
Demolished.

121 ESB Substation, Glebe Street,
Birr
Reg. 14819048

121 Mary Mother of God Roman
Catholic Church, Chapel Lane
Daingean
Reg. 14808014

122 Áras an Chontae, Charleville
Road, Tullamore
Not included in survey.

121 ESB Substation, Glebe Street,
Birr
Reg. 14819048

124 Crank House Visitor Centre,
Main Street, Banagher
Reg. 14810020

124 Gate Piers, Castropetre Church
of Ireland Church,
Church Walk,
Edenderry
Reg. 14804029

124 Head Gardener's House,
Charleville Demesne
Reg. 14917010

124 Gamekeeper's House,
Charleville Demesne
Reg. 14917012

Acknowledgements

NIAH
Senior Architect Willy Cumming
Survey Controller Mildred Dunne
GIS/IT Deborah Lawlor
NIAH Staff Damian Murphy, Gareth John,
Flora O'Mahony, TJ O'Meara, Barry O'Reilly,
Marc Ritchie, Joanne O'Riordan, Alan Murray,
Ann Kennedy and Emer Mulhall.

The NIAH gratefully acknowledges the following in the preparation of the Offaly County Survey and Introduction:

Survey Fieldwork
Architectural Recording & Research
(Sinead Hughes and Bronagh Lanigan).

Recorders
Sinead Hughes, Bronagh Langian, Caroline Healy,
Marie-Anne Lennon, Mary-Liz McCarthy, Niamh
McCullagh, Catherine Murphy and Róisín Quinn.

Introduction
Writer Jane Fenlon
Copy Editor Lucy Freeman
Photographer Nutan
Designed by Bennis Design
Printed by Brunswick Press

The NIAH wishes to thank all of those who allowed access to their property for the purpose of the County Offaly Survey and subsequent photography. The NIAH wishes to acknowledge the generous assistance given by the staff of the Photographic Section of the Department of the Environment, Heritage and Local Government, the Irish Architectural Archive, the National Library of Ireland, Aran O'Reilly of the National Photographic Archive; John Kearney and Michael Byrne of the Offaly Historic & Archaeological Society and Amanda Pedlow, Heritage Officer, Offaly County Council. Thanks also to Caimin O'Brien, Wendy Dunne and Donal Dunne.

Sources of Illustrations
All of the original photographs for the Introduction were taken by Nutan. The illustrations listed below are identified by their figure number:

1, 2, 3, 4, 5, 6 courtesy of the Photographic Section of the Department of the Environment, Heritage and Local Government; archival image on page 5 courtesy of the National Archives; 53, 60, 122, page 10, 86, 87, 111, 112 were taken by Architectural Recording and Research; 22, 36, 41, 74 , 94, 105, 116, 179, 181 are the property of the National Library of Ireland and have been reproduced with the permission of the Council of Trustees of the National Library of Ireland; 45, 72, 73, 100, 102, 103, 109, estate map page 82, images page 107 c/o The Birr Scientific and Heritage Foundation, courtesy of the Earl of Rosse; 57, 58, 67, 87, 88, 117, 159, archival image page 57 courtesy of the Irish Architectural Archive.

Please note that the majority of the structures included in the County Offaly Survey are privately owned and are therefore not open to the public.

ISBN: 0-7557-7174-5